Design with Color

A *Sunset* Design Guide

by Karen Templer and the Editors of Sunset Books

Contents

Color is one of the most important elements of any interior, and the surest way to inject your own personality into your living space. But many people find it a challenge. The aim of this book is not only to provide inspiration, but also to demystify the process of working with color. To that end, we've packed it full of smart advice—from the experts introduced on pages 4–5—and instructive case studies, along with hundreds of photos of successful interiors, ranging from neutral to subtle to over-the-top.

First, we'll introduce you to some basic terms, strategies, and concepts for working with color. Then, following an overview of the chief color families and their characteristics, we'll explore a range of methods for choosing, pairing, and employing colors. All in all, we'll give you the tools you need to create the rooms you want to live in.

34

76

©2009 by Sunset Publishing Corporation
80 Willow Road, Menlo Park, CA 94025

ISBN-13: 978-0-376-01350-7
ISBN-10: 0-376-01350-8
Library of Congress Control
Number: 2008942794

10 9 8 7 6 5 4 3 2 1
First Printing July 2009
Printed in the United States of America

OXMOOR HOUSE, INC.
VP, Publishing Director: Jim Childs
Brand Manager: Fonda Hitchcock
Managing Editor: L. Amanda Owens
Project Editor: Vanessa Lynn Rusch

Design with Color: A Sunset Design Guide
CONTRIBUTORS
Author: Karen Templer
Editor: Bob Doyle
Photo Editor: Cynthia Del Fava
Production Specialist: Linda M. Bouchard
Prepress Coordinator: Eligio Hernández
Copy Editor: Jacqueline Aaron
Principal Photographer: Michele Lee Willson
Principal Photo Stylist: Laura Del Fava
Intern: Emily Chappell
Indexer: Marjorie Joy
Series Designer: Vasken Guiragossian

To order additional publications,
call 1-800-765-6400

For more books to enrich your life,
visit **oxmoorhouse.com**

Visit Sunset online at **sunset.com**

For the most comprehensive selection of
Sunset books, visit **sunsetbooks.com**

For more exciting home and garden ideas,
visit **myhomeideas.com**

Cover Photo: Photography by Eric Roth;
design by Gayle Mandle Interior Design

Design Panel

The following design professionals from across the United States lent their enormous talent and valuable advice to the pages of this book.

Robin Bell
INTERIOR DESIGNER

An influential member of the international design community since 1983, Robin Bell is the principal of Robin Bell Design. Prior to opening her firm, she studied painting and drawing at the Art Students League of New York and worked in Sotheby's Decorative Works of Arts department. She was an assistant curator of the Gracie Mansion Conservancy, and was Senior Designer at McMillen Inc. Robin has appeared on CNN and has had her work featured in *Elle Decor, House Beautiful,* and other publications. One of her tables is in the permanent collection of the White House. **www.robinbelldesign.com** | *See an L.A. home by Robin on pages 114–115.*

Michael Bell
INTERIOR DESIGNER

In 2000, after 20 years of designing commercial interiors, Michael Bell started his firm, Michael K. Bell Interior Design Inc., specializing in high-end residential projects. He splits his time between his homes in Washington DC and Peaks Island, Maine, with clients in both locations. His work has appeared in *Metropolitan Home, Maine Home+Design,* and *Cottage Living.* His Washington DC home was featured on HGTV. | *See Michael's Maine cottage on pages 86–87 and 110.*

Tia Zoldan
INTERIOR DESIGNER

Tia Zoldan studied art and anthropology at the University of Arizona before embarking on a career in store design for J. Crew. She eventually settled in Los Angeles and, after helping numerous friends decorate their homes, opened Zoldan Interiors in 2004. She is continuously inspired by the beauty and architecture of L.A.'s historic homes, and her work has been featured in *Cottage Living.*
www.zoldaninteriors.com | *See Tia's own Los Angeles home on pages 31 (right), 64 (top right), and 152–153.*

John Lum, AIA
ARCHITECT

Principal of his own San Francisco firm, award-winning architect John Lum studied at Cal Poly and the École des Beaux-Arts. Since founding his firm in 1994, he has completed more than 400 projects, ranging from high-end retail spaces to residences, additions, and remodels. His projects are distinguished by their creative use of materials and form, and their vivid use of color. Lum and his team designed the 2007 *Sunset* Idea House, a major showcase for green technologies in the Bay Area.

www.johnlumarchitecture.com | *See John's work on pages 38, 111 (top right and bottom left), 146–147, 168–169, 175 (bottom right), and 184–185; and see his own San Francisco loft on pages 116–117.*

Lee Kleinhelter
RETAILER AND DESIGNER

Drawing on her background in interior design, Lee Kleinhelter opened Pieces in Atlanta's stylish Buckhead district in 2004. Pieces is a resource for furnishings that are clean-lined with a twist, mostly vintage items brought back to life. Lee's eye for color, composition, and unique combinations has caught the attention of *Elle Decor, Lucky, InStyle,* and the many other publications that have featured Pieces. Lee's own homes have been featured in *Cottage Living.* **www.piecesinc.com** | *See some of Lee's own rooms on pages 14 (center), 47 (left), 60 (bottom), and 163.*

Lisa Rowe
INTERIOR DESIGNER

Lisa Rowe was immersed in culture, art, and architecture at a very young age. She spent afternoons at the Philip Johnson–designed home of Houston art magnate Dominique de Menil—where her mother sorted through works by modern masters—and spent summers at her father's architectural firm, which provided her with a wealth of knowledge from the very best sources. In 1996, she founded Lisa Rowe Design, focusing on high-end residential projects. Her work has been published in *Southern Accents, InStyle Home, Cottage Living,* and other publications. | *See some of Lisa's own rooms on pages 43 (bottom), 64 (bottom left), 160, and 161 (top right).*

Carl Palasota
INTERIOR DESIGNER

With an interior design degree from Louisiana State University and 10 years of design experience in New York City, Carl Palasota returned home to Baton Rouge in 1989 to pilot his own firm. His mostly residential practice, with clients throughout the country, has been recognized in a variety of publications, including *Southern Accents, House & Garden UK,* and *Cottage Living.* | *See Carl's work on pages 10 (top left), 43 (top right), 71 (top left), 78, and 102 (bottom right); and see his own Louisiana cottage on pages 77 and 92–93.*

Charles De Lisle
DESIGNER

An interior, product, and furniture designer, Charles De Lisle helps his clients find a good fit between the location, environment, and architecture of any given site. Trained in ceramics, sculpture, and architecture, Charles has taken his formal arts background and talent for seeing the three-dimensional world with imagination and detail, and translated them into a career designing interiors for residences and hotels in California, Hawaii, New York, Seattle, and Montana. His work has been published in *Sunset, Interior Design, Dwell,* and the *New York Times Magazine,* among others. **www.dpsinteriors.com** | *See Charles's work on pages 10 (bottom right), 100 (top), 106 (top right and bottom right), 108, 111 (bottom right), 122–123, 126–127, 148–149, 157 (bottom right), and 172–173.*

Chapter 1

Introduction to Color

It can fairly be said that color is part science and part art, but neither part needs to be intimidating. In this first chapter, we'll introduce you to some basic concepts and strategies that will serve as a frame of reference for you throughout the book. The more you know about how color works, the easier you'll find it to work with, whether you're decorating your own home or preparing for conversations with an architect or a designer. As any good professional will tell you, the most important thing about the color in your home is that it be a reflection of *you*.

Color Basics

It's true that there's an element of science to color, in the sense that color is a function of refracted light and its perception by the human eye. But it's not *rocket* science. As architect John Lum says, "There's a lot of mystique around color and color consultants, but I don't think it takes an expert to understand color." What it does take is a little bit of study coupled with the ability to trust your judgment.

Goals and Preferences

Perhaps the best place to start when tackling the questions of how and where to use color in your rooms is to ask yourself what you want from your home.

Generally speaking, color is energy. The brighter or more saturated the colors, the more energy they impart. And how energetic a home should feel is entirely a matter of personal preference. Are you the kind who wants your home to feel like a soothing retreat from a noisy world, an energizing and inspiring environment in and of itself, or something in between? The more aware you are of your *motivation*, the better decisions you'll make. Are you a big fan of color, looking for ways to incorporate more and more of it into your life? Are you living in low-color rooms, wanting them to have a bit more *oomph*? And what about the scope of your project? Are you on a mission to change everything or just jazz it up a little bit? At the outset, these are more important issues than the question of which colors to use. About *that*, it's important to keep an open mind—at least for the time being.

LEFT Do you want your home to be bold and dramatic, quiet and soothing, or perhaps bright and cheery like this family room?

"I find, generally, that people are not aware of how they feel about color until the process evolves," says designer Robin Bell. "People are very opinionated about color, more than anything else in the design process, and they'll come in with specific prejudices about colors. It is important to establish early on that it's not about a color; it's about the *relationship* of colors." In other words, it's about the effect the colors have on your room (and hence, on you). As an analogy, she cites the common occurrence of people thinking they know exactly what style of house they want, only to walk into one they never thought they'd like and find themselves in love with it. "I had one client, for example, who said, 'The one color I hate is orange.' The last room we did was the master bedroom, and at the end of the day, after I'd proposed all sorts of things, the bedroom is bright orange and white, and she's thrilled with it."

Designer and shop owner Lee Kleinhelter agrees that people who are open to being surprised are often the happier for it, and that goes as much for the volume of color as the hue. "I think often people just need to be exposed to more," she says. "When they come into my store and realize that a punch of color can be used in a simple way, that it can make an impact and not be a huge commitment, they tell us all the time that they feel inspired." So the best place to start is to think about how you want your home to feel, rather than what colors you want it to be, and to let go of any preconceived notions about good or bad colors. Even if you're embarking on a project with a palette of colors already in mind, try to allow for some spontaneity along the way.

Finding Inspiration

To zero in on your objectives, the best exercise is to look at photos and see what you respond to—without thinking about color, per se, just reacting to the rooms. Flip through the images in this book and a magazine or two, and flag anything that makes you feel the way you want your rooms to make you feel. Robin Bell says a picture is worth a thousand words: "I ask my clients to bring in five tear sheets of interiors they absolutely adore, instinctively—regardless of whether the rooms have anything to do with their project—and two that they can't stand. Once you've got images in front of you, you can look for clues." She looks for whether there's harmony or contrast, a lot or a little color, and how that color is used. "People who like serenity are going to pick rooms where there aren't a lot of jarring accents. People interested in a lot of panache and drama are going to pick rooms with more contrast. There's a tendency to focus on the specific, but it's important to take a longer view."

Once you've got your photos flagged, look for the commonalities. Is there harmony or contrast? Is the color dominant or recessive? How much color is there, and what are some of the surface materials? How would you describe the mood of the rooms? Designers Robin Bell and Charles De Lisle both note that what clients bring them in the way of images is very often different from what they've said they like. You might find that the rooms you've responded to are more colorful or less colorful than you thought you preferred, or that color has been used in a different way than you would have expected.

TOP LEFT Deeper colors create more dramatic settings, as in this bedroom by Carl Palasota.

BOTTOM LEFT Soft colors, like those of the walls, curtains, and ottoman in this sitting room, create a calm environment.

TOP RIGHT Used in unexpected ways—like a chair and window trim in a matching hue—a little bit of color creates a big impact.

BOTTOM RIGHT Charles De Lisle balanced the bright colors in this room with lots of wood, resulting in a somewhat subdued effect.

Making It Personal

As much as color is subject to fashion, it is primarily a means of personal expression. For most people, the best solution is one that reflects their wishes and personality rather than one that reflects current trends. Lee Kleinhelter notes, "What's in and hot now won't be tomorrow. A home needs to be about what the owner responds to and what they want to look at every day."

"I'm working with a woman now who is just not a beige person," says designer Michael Bell. "She wants her house to reflect her," and he agrees that's how it ought to be. He finds a lot of his clients fearful about color in the beginning, but, he says, "a typical response in the end is, 'I would never have thought to use that color on the walls, but I love how it looks and how I feel in it.'" For all of these designers, the best reason to use any particular color is that you simply love that hue.

So how do you begin to find your favorites? In addition to studying photographs of other people's rooms, there are some clues to be found closer to home. For many people, the biggest indicator of color comfort level and preferences is their wardrobe. "I have one client who loves jewel tones and wears these intense blues and purples," says John Lum. "She and her husband have responded when we show them those colors, which is a clear signal."

Michael Bell says, "A lot of clients, if I ask them outright what colors they like, they have a hard time verbalizing it. But if I ask them what they wear, it's easier for them to talk about their preferences."

Carl Palasota often responds to a client's physical traits. "I look at what they wear, but also what they would look good in. I have a client who has this very striking platinum hair and silvery-violet eyes. I said 'violet' in a meeting and she responded." Another client is Vietnamese, with incredible dark-brown hair. "I didn't really think, *I'm going to repeat the color of her hair,* but we created a space for her that's full of these beautiful grays and stainless steel, with bronze doors, and she just looks amazing in it. She's the object in her space. I would hope we would all look that good in our surroundings."

You might also find clues already in your home. Is there a piece of art that you love and want to use? Perhaps you have a collection—shells or beach glass or pottery—that you're attracted to in part because of the colors. Maybe you've simply had a favorite color for as long as you can remember. Gather these influences and keep them in mind.

Strategic Thinking

A room's color might come in the form of paint, flooring, rugs, wallpaper, tile, upholstery, accessories, artwork, or all of the above. So where do you begin? There aren't any rules, but there are some helpful strategies.

The traditional advice is to start with a patterned textile—a rug or a fabric—

and pull your colors from there. "There are so many more paint colors than fabric colors," says Tia Zoldan. "If I'm looking through a color wheel and I find a beautiful mauve and try to go out and find fabric to match, it's pretty hard. It's much easier to match a paint to a fabric." For that reason, Michael Bell says wall colors are usually one of the last things

he picks—unless he plans to use a wallpaper, in which case it will come first. Robin Bell, on the other hand, always starts with the wall color. Her focus is on creating dynamic relationships between patterns and colors, and sometimes nothing else in the room is the same color as the walls. For her, the wall color's job is to set the tone. "Very often

LEFT If you've got coordinating fabrics, it's easy to have a paint color custom-tinted to match.

RIGHT When rooms open into one another, make sure the wall colors complement each other.

it fades back into nothing—you might not even notice the room is yellow." Even if you're using a textile as your jumping-off point, consider picking lighter or darker shades rather than matching the colors precisely.

Carl Palasota reinforces Robin Bell's message: "It's all about how things relate to each other and speak to one another."

That also goes for adjacent rooms: "A lot of people will paint their homes willy-nilly," says John Lum. "You need to have a sense of how the rooms flow, the relationship of rooms, so you don't have colors clashing. You also want to balance it so you don't have too much color in one part of the house and then none anywhere else."

"Depending on how large a space is and how the architecture breaks up, I'll sometimes do a gradation of colors rather than a total change," says Michael Bell. "I might use colors of similar value—maybe gray-green in one room and a gray-blue in the next. Or I'll take the wall color and make it deeper in one room, lighter in another." (Carl Palasota notes that paint cards, with their rows of slightly shifting shades, offer an easy way for a novice to pick subtle pairings.) Charles De Lisle tends to use color within the room rather than on the wall, and prefers the relationships to be slightly less harmonious. "I like subtly

jarring colors—like using sky blue in one room, and then in the next room it's a little bit greener, and then in the next it's olive." Another strategy Michael Bell uses is to pick three colors—a dominant color, a recessive color, and an accent color—and then switch the hierarchy of them around from one room to the next.

Tia Zoldan's strategy is similar, picking five or six colors and using them in varying ways. "I don't go from one color story to a complete opposite. Say I have kelly-green pillows on a couch and want to do something vibrant for the hallway; I might repeat that green. So it's not random—one room leads to the next." Another of her favorite tricks has to do with ceiling and trim color. "If I'm using a dark color on the walls, I like to keep the ceiling white. But if I'm using a soft color, like a neutral taupey gray, I think it looks so pretty and soothing if you do the ceiling and trim in a lighter shade of the same color."

How Much, For How Long

A big determinant for how and where you use color is the longevity factor: how long will you like it and what will it take to change it? Michael Bell and John Lum both note that paint creates the most bang for the buck. "It's the least expensive way to get a lot of effect, and it's relatively easy to change if you get tired of it. So paint is fantastic for introducing color," says Bell. Repainting kitchen cabinets is a bigger chore than repainting an accent wall, but likely easier than reupholstering a sofa. "People are nervous to invest thousands of dollars in a good sofa if it's orange," Bell says. "They're more likely to invest in a beige sofa," and bring in the orange some other way.

Despite the relative ease and impact of colored walls, many of our design panelists like a neutral backdrop. Charles De Lisle says it's "pretty rare" for him to paint a whole room a color. Lisa Rowe has noticed that, in recent years, her clients have been more open to the use of color in general. "When I first started, the monochromatic look was very in." But, she says, "I still keep most of the major pieces in my interiors neutral

THIS PAGE You may know you want green in a room, but which shade, how much of it, and in what form?

OPPOSITE PAGE Paint is a relatively inexpensive way to completely transform a space.

while injecting a pop of color through cushions, lamps, and art." Michael Bell and Tia Zoldan both like to do some colored upholstery, but find it's often best to keep it to smaller pieces—a side chair or an ottoman. The simplest sources of color are accessories: throw pillows, lamps, rugs, anything that you can pick up and replace any day. Some people are more comfortable with the lower commitment of that, and others simply want the freedom to change things as often as they like.

"I think there's a lot of fear of things going out of style," says Bell. "I tell my clients, if you like these colors now, I think you're still going to like them in five or ten years." But he notes that he's in Washington, DC, where most people don't stay in the same place that long. Similarly, Charles De Lisle remarks that what he does with a second home is likely to be bolder and more whimsical than what he'd do in a house people live in year-round.

DESIGNER
LISA ROWE ON

The Big Picture

Lisa Rowe thinks the most important thing about working with color is having an overall palette and strategy in mind. "It is so much nicer to be in a space that, while the color may shift from room to room, it all has a cohesiveness. Not that I don't like to inject something unexpected, like an emerald-green lacquered dining room, but it needs to be thoughtful."

Consulting the Color Wheel

Fortunately, choosing colors for your home needn't be all intuition or guesswork. Pretty much anyone who has studied art and design of any kind started with a class in color theory, which began with an introduction to the color wheel. For most professionals, the wheel and its uses become instinctive, but some continue to refer to it when looking for a solution or inspiration.

The wheel is a visual representation of the color spectrum, demonstrating how colors relate to each other. When you were a kid, you probably learned the mnemonic for remembering the order of colors in a rainbow: Roy G. Biv—that is, red, orange, yellow, green, blue, indigo, violet. But the spectrum is actually circular—violet (otherwise known as purple) loops back around to red. On page 186, you'll find a larger version of the wheel at right, along with a glossary of terms. As you proceed through this book, we'll explore all of these concepts in more detail, but following are the fundamentals.

One half of the wheel is made up of *warm* colors—from red-violet through the reds and oranges to yellow. The other half—yellow-green through violet—are the *cool* colors.

There are three *primary* colors—essentially, the colors from which all other colors derive. These are red, yellow, and blue. (If you drew a line connecting them on the wheel, you'd have a triangle.) When you blend any two primary colors together, you get a *secondary* color: yellow and blue make green, blue and red make purple, red and yellow make orange. So those are the secondary colors: green, purple, and orange. Mix a primary and a secondary color and you get a *tertiary* color: red and orange make red-orange, orange and yellow make yellow-orange, and so on.

When we talk about color—or *hue*—we also talk about its *value* or *saturation*. Colors of the same value are found on the same rung of the wheel. A saturated color is one with a lot of pigment. Candy serves as a good example here: standard M&M's colors are of the same value as each other, all fairly saturated colors. Jordan almonds, on the other hand, are all pastels—again, all of equal (in this case, low) saturation. Adding white to any color makes it progressively lighter, or less saturated. Adding black makes it darker. Lighter and darker versions of the same color are *shades*. Add a drop of black to a pastel and you'll get a grayer version of that color—like mauve instead of pale pink, or sage instead of mint green.

There are a few simple methods for creating color palettes based on colors' relative positions on the wheel. Colors that are side-by-side are called *analogous*. Colors that are directly opposite each other are called *complements*. The colors to either side of any color's complement would be its *split complements*. (See Chapters 4 and 5 for more on all of this.) Until you are comfortable combining colors freely, using these relationships to come up with combinations is helpful.

Of course, you're also free to simply look at a color wheel and pick out colors you like, regardless of where they fall. Designer Tia Zoldan loves color wheels, paint-swatch fan decks, and fabric samples. "I love all colors," she says. "I go crazy over combinations, and I love to try to think of new ones. It's so much more exciting to walk into a room and not see the same old stagnant colors that everyone uses. So I'll sit at home with my color wheel and my fabrics and put random colors together and think, *Whoa, I have to use that!* There aren't enough rooms!"

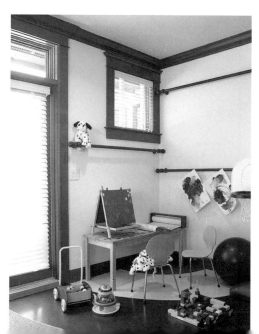

RIGHT AND OPPO-SITE PAGE Red, blue, and yellow are the building blocks of color and, as such, are a popular palette for kids' spaces. They are used in more sophisticated shades for this very grown-up bedroom.

The Power of Color

Color is not a passive element in a room. It calls attention to itself, and as such, it has power. It can define space, direct attention, emphasize features, form a focal point. And most of all, it creates a mood.

Augmenting the Architecture

"Color can change the architectural perception of a room," says Robin Bell. "For instance, if you have small rooms with very high ceilings, that can create a tunnel effect. If you have molding at a picture-rail line—or you simply create a line where the picture rail would be—you can paint a color just from that point down, and you have an immediate architectural change. If you have an undistinguished doorway, paint a border around it with color and it will create a more imposing perception. The same with windows." If, on the other hand, you have beautiful doors and moldings, or other features you'd like to play up, painting them a seductive color—or simply painting them white where the walls are a color—will call attention to them.

The opposite is also true. Light and shadow are what allow us to make out forms. Nothing shows a shadow better than white. So if you've got damaged, uneven, or pockmarked walls, painting them white will allow you to see every little flaw. The darker you paint them, the less evident the shadows, the less apparent the flaws. (This is the same reason so many people love black pants—any bulges and wrinkles are relatively lost in the shadows.)

Directing Attention

You can also use color to define space or direct people's attention through it. In the same way you'd use an area rug to create a more intimate setting within a large room, you can use an accent wall to anchor a group of furnishings. Painting rooms the same color can make a small house feel larger by making it feel like one cohesive space instead of a sequence of small ones. In a larger house, you can use wall colors to create definition and shifting moods from one room to the next. For an open-plan space, such as a loft, it can be especially important to create a focal point or series of focal points, to impart a sense of organization and purpose. Again, this might come in the form of a wall color, or it might be a boldly upholstered piece of furniture or a brilliant rug or bedspread.

OPPOSITE PAGE Avocado-green paint gives this room instant character and emphasizes its most interesting feature.

TOP Midnight-blue paint makes for a dramatic entryway. It also highlights the beautiful white doors and molding.

BOTTOM LEFT AND RIGHT The dark-brown accent wall directs your attention down the hallway, defines a library seating area, and accentuates the shape of the room.

Even in easy-to-swap accessories, a change of color scheme alters a room's mood.

Setting a Mood

Color and mood go hand in hand, which is why it's important not to get too attached to the idea of any particular color before you've determined what you want to accomplish. It's not enough to know, for example, that you want a blue room. As Robin Bell points out, "that could mean a snappy, naval blue-and-white room, or it could mean serene, soggy, sea-glass colors. Both 'blue,' but two totally different moods. If you think you want blue, it's very important to determine whether that means you want a blue background or you want objects to read as blue in the room."

You might also have a color in mind that's not well suited to your goal. For instance, your favorite color in the world might be orange, but your goal might be to create a restful place for yourself. Orange is about as energetic as a color gets, so perhaps you'll want to use it only as an accent with a lot of neutrals to calm it down. Or maybe you'll opt to use a dark, earthy orange or a pale salmon.

In trying to get color and mood in alignment, saturation matters as much as the hue. Again, the brighter a color is, the more energy it lends a room. Paler or deeper colors are calmer and will contribute that calmness.

John Lum likes to work with bright colors in controlled ways, and finds some clients reluctant at first. "Someone might think they don't want lime green in their home, but as we show them the other materials that surround the lime green, they see that it gives energy to the space." Think in terms of matching colors' saturation level to the energy level you want for your room, and about how you can achieve just the right balance.

Bear in mind, too, that colors have temperature. As noted on page 16, colors with a lot of purple, blue, or green to them are cool in nature, while yellows, oranges, and reds are warm. If you live in a warm climate, you might enjoy using a lot of hot, tropical colors—bright pinks and fiery oranges. On the other hand, you might want your home to be a cool retreat from the heat, in which case you'd want to use lots of watery blues and greens.

One critical aspect of working with color is often overlooked by non-professionals: the impact of light. Light has a potentially dramatic effect on how a color will look in a given room, but the considerations don't end there.

Light Color

Most people have heard the advice about testing colors in your home, particularly wall colors, but few heed it. The simple fact is, you could paint three different rooms the exact same color and find that they look completely different. That's because all light—natural or artificial—has its own color. (Just think of the greenish cast many people associate with compact fluorescent bulbs versus the more yellow incandescent light we're accustomed to.) The color of the light affects the perception of whatever it's illuminating, whether that's a couch, a painting, or a wall. Also, light changes over the course of the day. A color that reads beautifully in morning sunlight might become muddy in the afternoon or turn garish under lamplight in the evening. A paint color that looks perfect under the daylight-balanced lights of the paint-store display may look completely different in your living room. To get the same color you're seeing in the store, you might need to use a color from two or three shades up or down the chart. The only way to know for sure is to take things home and try them out.

"Fortunately," says designer Michael Bell, "the way the market has developed, virtually all of the paint manufacturers now offer sample jars, and that's fantastic because often I'll take a bunch for a client and we'll paint big swatches in various rooms so they can get a sense of how the color will really look, and how it changes through the day—and also how the spaces will relate to each other." If you want multiple rooms to appear to be the identical color, you might have to vary the paint choice slightly from room to room. On the other hand, using the same color in differing light conditions can be an easy way to create a subtle shift from one room to the next—so long as you like the way it looks in each case. As Carl Palasota points out, the most interesting colors may be those that shift the most: "colors that slowly unfold instead of 'wow, it's red.'"

OPPOSITE PAGE White walls and gleaming floors make the most of ample daylight, bouncing it around the space.

ABOVE RIGHT It's important to audition colors in the space where they'll be used, to make sure they work with your light.

DESIGNER
ROBIN BELL ON

Reflective Surfaces

The two most highly reflective surfaces in a room are the ceiling and the floor," says Robin Bell. "We have the ability to grab light and work with it using our floors and ceilings." White ceilings and polished floors, for instance, are like "giant reflectors."

ABOVE LEFT Golden-yellow walls and bright white trim create the illusion of a sun-drenched space.

ABOVE RIGHT Plenty of natural light shows this soft-green tile to its best advantage.

Light Quantity and Quality

Generally speaking, white and other light colors reflect light—brightening a space—while dark colors absorb it, but there are mitigating factors. The *quantity* and *quality* of light both need to be taken into account.

Where many of our design panelists take color cues from their clients first, Los Angeles designer Tia Zoldan takes hers from the house. "I feel like I can walk into a house and, depending on the light and the way the house sits in relation to the sun, how the light filters, I can see whether it can use a lot of color, and whether they'll be lighter or darker colors. I have a lot more options with a brighter room." New Yorker Robin Bell concurs. She works

on both city and country homes—two very different situations where light is concerned. "One of the trickiest things to accomplish is a successful color scheme in low-light conditions—hallways, bathrooms, New York City apartments. The common perception is that you should paint it all white or a soft pastel, that you can't go dark. But in low-light conditions, it's contrast or brilliance that creates the impression of light. If you take a color with a lot of punch and combine it with white, you create the sensation of brightness. On the other hand, if you pick a color in a mid-pale range, like a pretty pastel, it reads dingy and depressing." In a room with little daylight, even white can appear dishwater gray. However, she says: "In the country, where you have

lots of warm, yellow, favorable light, you can use all kinds of lovely soft colors—even very drab colors—and they look spectacular. That light will create a reaction in those wall colors."

Similarly, Charles De Lisle works with clients in both Northern California and Hawaii, and finds that colors he's accustomed to using in California don't stand up to Hawaiian light. "The light in California is buttery and a lot warmer. It has a different mood to it. You don't have to use a lot of color to get color out of something. In Hawaii the light is brighter, sharper, more shadowy, and it feels more blue." Not only do very bright colors stand up to this light, it demands them—subtler shades get washed out. De Lisle has also repainted rooms because the light

turned the colors blue-green. "We've had to push things more yellow to counteract that blueness." He recently completed his first project in Montana, which was a different story altogether. "The client didn't want the stereotypical Montana home—black and red and antlers—so we ended up looking at what the colors are out there. It has this moody purpleness to it, so we did slate blues and lavender, which I've never done in California."

ABOVE LEFT A good strategy for low light is to use a bright, clear color plus white trim.

ABOVE RIGHT Chocolate brown, which absorbs light, turns this covered porch into a refuge from the coastal sun.

Texture and Finish

Variations in surface character take two general forms: texture (for example, stuccoed, woven, furry) and finish (matte, weathered, polished). Texture and finish impact a room in two ways: they affect the perception of color, and they create visual interest.

Color and Character

In the same way that a single color can look different under varying light conditions, so can it look different with variations in texture and finish—and light plays a key role in this. Picture matte black paint and black patent leather, or brown wood and brown velvet. "A woven surface absorbs light," Robin Bell explains, while "a smooth or shiny surface reflects light. So the same color in two different finishes will look different." Carl Palasota offers the example of his own hand-troweled plaster walls, which have a mottled and dappled character. "We could never get that same color with paint. But the question of finish is just as important at the other extreme, like with perfectly smooth, seamless walls that are lacquered to a high gloss. Perfection can be as intriguing and wonderful playing into a palette as imperfection can. Texture plays a part in both directions."

From a practical standpoint, it's important to keep this in mind when, for instance, you're looking at paint colors. If the paint chip is matte and you'll be buying glossy paint, the color won't look the same. Or if you're planning to have the walls glazed after they're painted, that will affect the intensity of the color. So again, test a few different shades.

From a design standpoint, though, texture and finish are tools you can use to add another layer of character to a room. Even if you're working with a single color, using it in a range of materials and textures will create the perception of subtle shifts in color. Says Robin Bell, "Texture sets a mood: one plays off another just as colors do. It would not be a good idea for everything in the room to have the same texture—everything's a linen weave, or everything's shiny. Much in the way dark and light colors relate positively, so does a smooth texture and a very nubby one, for example. They play very well against each other. It's important to have a play of textures, a play of colors, *and* a play of finishes. All three work hand in hand."

OPPOSITE PAGE Although they're the same color, the velvet of the settee has more depth and variation than the headboard fabric.

ABOVE Luxe chocolate-brown furniture and matte mocha-colored walls complement each other beautifully.

RIGHT A plaster wall and weathered cupboard offer intriguing variations in color and surface character.

BELOW An array of textures and finishes—here, a glossy white ceiling and sisal floor, wicker furniture and cotton slipcovers— is especially important in a neutral space (see Chapter 3).

LEFT Converting a living room to a pool room is a bold move. Papering it in a large-scale, black-and-white pattern is an even bolder one.

RIGHT If you are unsure about working with pattern, throw pillows are always a good method to ease your way in.

Color doesn't only come in solids and textures, of course. There's also the matter of pattern. While there are a lot of color-shy people in the world, pattern can feel like an even bigger hurdle—or an even more personal means of expression. Use of pattern can make a significant difference in a space, and it can be as simple as a checkerboard floor or as complex as an intricate palette of differently patterned elements.

Types and Forms

As you can see from the photos in this section and throughout the book, pattern runs the gamut—everything from stripes to geometrics to animal prints to florals and scenics. They come in neutrals and colors. And they range from the dainty florals of a classic Liberty print to very large-scale paisleys or wide awning stripes. What's more, you have the wide diversity of forms that patterns can take. There are tile patterns (and patterned tiles) for floors, counters, and walls. Patterned fabrics might be put to use as pillows, upholstery, drapes, tablecloths, or wall coverings. Paint can be applied in any pattern you can dream up and tape off—stripes, plaids, color blocks, polka dots—anywhere from the floor to the furniture to the ceiling. And then there are the wallpapers. The possibilities are truly endless.

Focal Point or Accent

So how much pattern is the right amount? And how do you pick pattern that will work for you? As Robin Bell puts it, "I don't think there are any rules of good or bad pattern. It's a question of personal preference." Some people are just more comfortable with solids, but what pattern does for a room—even in very small doses—is liven things up. It gives the eye a place to linger. A large swath of a bold pattern instantly animates a space, while a smaller hit or a subtler pattern simply creates a little interest. Whether you'll use pattern as an accent or a focal point is strictly a matter of your goals, your taste, and your comfort level.

Tia Zoldan doesn't think of herself as a big user of pattern: "I like a traditional stripe," she says. "If I do pattern in a room, I might do it on one chair, just as a little focal point. But I don't like overly patterned rooms." Charles De Lisle, on the other hand, is an enthusiast: "I'm from the East Coast, and I have this Yankee aesthetic ingrained in me. I'm really attracted to very classic prints—block prints, tea-stained prints, Liberty prints with the flowers. I love that stuff." He also creates a lot of original patterns for clients and does inventive things with them—printing bright inks on hemp, or photographs on silk, and using them on everything from walls to cabinets. Don't be afraid to experiment. But, as with color in general, keep in mind how permanent the application of the pattern is and how long you can expect to like what you've come up with. If you decide you want red-and-white stripes, for instance, a tiled backsplash is bigger statement—and an even bigger commitment—than, say, an upholstered chair.

THIS PAGE, TOP A diamond pattern painted in black on the wood floor amplifies this kitchen's retro personality.

THIS PAGE, BOTTOM A single, one-color print makes a strong statement when repeated on a folding screen, an armchair, and a bedskirt.

OPPOSITE PAGE, TOP Mix-and-match patterned tiles turn ordinary kitchen cabinets into something special.

OPPOSITE PAGE, BOTTOM LEFT AND RIGHT The impact of wallpaper depends on the paper—the strength of the color and pattern—and how much of it you use.

DESIGNER
TIA ZOLDAN ON

Risk and Reward

I have the resources to change my house a lot, but obviously my clients aren't going to change things as often," says Tia Zoldan. "So whatever pattern I use for others, I typically do it in small, small doses. But because I use pattern in a way that's easy to change, it also frees me up to be riskier with the use of it, and with the combinations." Taking some risks is ultimately what will make your room feel unique.

Mixing with Confidence

Some of the most dynamic rooms are those that combine patterns in creative and confident ways. Again, there aren't any rules to get hung up on, but there is some conventional wisdom. "I like to use a lot of pattern," says Michael Bell, "and I mix patterns. Generally, I think if you start with a big pattern, you can mix it with a smaller pattern and a geometric—a stripe, a check—and with some solid texture. I think it comes down to scale: use patterns of a different scale, balancing organics with geometrics and, again, mixing that with texture. So it's not all pattern and flat color." Carl Palasota likes to start with a stripe and/or a check before working in something more organic, but he also likes to keep control over the mix by limiting the color, thereby maintaining an overall calmness. As always, it goes back to the question of how complex or simple, exuberant or relaxing, you want a room to be.

OPPOSITE PAGE The old-school look requires lots of casually layered patterns, as with this wall tapestry, geometric rug, and loose mix of small-scale patterns on the upholstery and pillow fabrics.

ABOVE A more modern look depends on a crisper combination, like this ticking stripe, plaid, and zebra print—all in shades of black, white, and brown.

RIGHT The Hollywood Regency revivalists combine large-scale patterns and bold geometrics with lots of bright color.

Chapter 2

Color Profiles

Do you have a favorite color? Most people do—for some of us it hasn't changed since childhood—but few of us have ever really considered what it is about our favorite that makes it so appealing. Are you making a statement? Responding to a trend? Or are you reacting to the color on an emotional level? A little bit of understanding about the basic colors and their impact can go a long way when it comes to choosing hues and shades, and combining them successfully.

White can be soft and romantic, glossy and modern, or just about anything in between. Technically, white is the absence of color, but the notion of pure white is almost a myth. The fact is essentially every white has an undertone—it may tip toward yellow, pink, or blue. If you've ever shopped for white paint, you've seen the multitude of paint chips ranging from icy blue-white to the color of fresh cream. White is also where finish and texture have perhaps the biggest impact. Just think of the difference between a weathered or hand-rubbed white-painted cabinet and one in glossy white lacquer: even if the whites are exactly the same color, the impact is entirely different.

When using a lot of white, it can be helpful to use several shades, but be careful that you're using all warm or all cool shades: one white can make another white look perfectly blue. Combining them—perhaps chalk-white walls with a creamier trim—can add depth to a space, making it look more refined than whitewashed.

In smaller doses, white can still have a subtle yet significant impact. In a room full of soft, warm shades, for instance, a spot of bright white—a table, or the piping on a chair—can snap things into focus, keeping the overall scheme from looking muddy.

OPPOSITE PAGE White is the first choice of modernists and minimalists; it shows off the architecture rather than competing with it.

ABOVE Crisp white beds look luminous in a room of stone and wood.

RIGHT White on every surface, including the floor, makes a bathroom as bright and clean-looking as possible.

BELOW Mixing shades and textures of white creates a layered look—here it's soft cotton, woven nylon webbing, and hard lacquer.

DESIGNER
LEE KLEINHELTER ON

Loving White

Although she's known for pops of bright, clear color, Kleinhelter's favorite color is white. "It's just me. I think most things look better white," she says. "But it has to be the right white: not too cold and sterile, but also not off-white. It's like a canvas, and I think it makes a space feel much larger—fresh and clean." She adds, "If I could wear my white jeans in the winter, I would."

Blue

Fields of two very different blue tiles—pale-aqua glass and deep-blue textured ceramic—provide cool contrast to the warm teak.

If you were to poll the populace on their favorite colors, it's a safe bet that blue would come up the winner. It has been demonstrated that blue has a calming effect: people feel more content sitting in a room with cerulean or cornflower-blue walls. And blue is arguably the easiest color to work with. As a nation of people who live in jeans, we're well practiced at pairing blue with just about anything, whether we realize it or not. On many levels, we're simply *comfortable* with blue.

So in the "goes with anything" sense of the word, blue is a neutral, but not all blues are alike. Take true blue and add an abundance of white, and you get "baby blue"—an association that's difficult to avoid. Shift it toward gray-blue or blue-green, though, and you've got something more sophisticated to work with. Navy has its own connotations, from ships and sailors to the classic navy business suit. In other words, its effect tends to be more grown-up and polished. Turquoise blues, on the other hand, have an innately exotic character.

Coastal homes are commonly decorated in blue and white—either to achieve a nautical effect, to mirror the sky-and-water surroundings, or to capitalize on blue's cool character in hot climates. But in settings where blue can feel too chilly, it helps to reach across the color wheel and find some warmer tones to balance the effect. When using red with blue, the challenge is to avoid a patriotic look (unless, of course, that's what you're going for). Blue's complement is orange, but blue and orange can be a jarring duo. The trick is to pick your shades carefully: consider combinations like deep orange with turquoise; navy blue with a soft sherbet shade; or a bright, citrusy orange with a pale, icy blue. Medium blue with buttery yellow, meanwhile, is a timeless combination, and one especially evocative of the French-country style. Easily

the most popular color pairing in recent years is blue and brown, particularly robin's-egg blue combined with multiple shades of brown. The ubiquity of it makes it seem boring to a bold colorist like designer Tia Zoldan, but it's a mix with undeniably wide appeal, and a relatively easy one to pull off.

TOP LEFT Even the most basic couch becomes a conversation piece when covered in polished, quilted sapphire blue.

TOP RIGHT Navy and white nautical stripes are always popular in coastal homes.

BOTTOM LEFT A single weathered-blue Windsor chair adds a touch of charm to this mix.

BOTTOM RIGHT Slate-blue walls make sense in an older-boys' room that doubles as a guest room.

TOP LEFT Blue and brown make for a soothing combination, perfect for a master bedroom.

TOP RIGHT Blue and its complement, orange, are used together here in slightly less saturated shades—the softer side of bold.

BOTTOM LEFT An assortment of patterned pillows lightens up a conservative navy and red scheme.

BOTTOM RIGHT A robin's-egg blue door is a pleasant surprise.

OPPOSITE PAGE A bright turquoise stool and daybed (dressed in blue ticking stripes) are standouts on a dark-red porch.

Red

As color temperature goes, red is as hot as it gets. Just as with blue, there are people who consider red a neutral and will pair it with everything. But then, there isn't just one red. Reds range from red-red-violet to red-orange. Lighten red and you get pink; darken it and you get brick or burgundy. Some people consider it paramount to match reds perfectly, while others enjoy seeing pink-red, blue-red, and orange-red all playing off of each other; it is strictly a matter of taste. However, when using red on walls, it's especially important to test it in the space and in varying light conditions—it's all too common to end up with a pinker or bluer red than what you had in mind.

Unlike blue, red isn't for everyone, but hot-natured people tend to gravitate to it. Architect John Lum notes that red is symbolic of good luck in Asian cultures, and he's had clients request its use for that reason. Keep in mind, too, that it is an advancing color, meaning it will appear to pop out of any scene. That makes it ideal for creating a focal point or directing attention, and means it is effective even in small doses. Red's complement is green. To avoid the Christmas look, think sage or chartreuse.

OPPOSITE PAGE This dining room is layered with red in multiple shades and patterns, for a sophisticated effect.

TOP LEFT A red floor starts any room off on a dramatic foot.

TOP RIGHT Painted cherry red and flanked by pearl-gray doors, a grandfather clock is anything but stuffy.

BOTTOM Red accents add considerable punch to a light-blue boys' room.

LEFT Even a small dose of red—here in a romantic floral print—enlivens an otherwise neutral room.

TOP A slightly glossy red feels right at home in this Colonial house.

BOTTOM LEFT The red door sounds an Asian note on the front of a modernist home.

BOTTOM RIGHT Bold red-leather office chairs anchor this soaring dining space.

Although it's consistently described in terms like *sunny*, *warm*, and *cheery*, yellow enjoys less universal appeal than the other primary colors. Particularly in fashion and interiors, it tends to come and go, much more so than red or blue. Yellow has a fairly wide range, from the palest pastel to bright lemon to deep mustard. And because it sits between a hot color (orange) and a cool color (green), yellow's mood can change depending on where it falls in the spectrum: yellow-orange is warmer than yellow-green. Even more subject to trends than yellow itself is what it's paired with. Red and yellow is a combination considered verboten by many (which can make it unexpected and interesting), although a spicy combination of the analogous hot hues of red, orange, and yellow is common in Latin quarters. Yellow and green was

an extremely popular combo in the '70s, so it was simply not done for many years thereafter; now it looks fresh again. The same goes for yellow and brown. Yellow's complement is purple—a combination that's extremely popular in gardens but not so much indoors, though yellow and blue is a fairly timeless mix. But one of the hottest combinations in recent years is yellow with gray, a lovely warm-cool pairing.

While yellow walls can indeed make a room feel sunny, be careful about the shade you choose and where you use it. It's popular in kitchens and bedrooms—both spaces where sunny seems like a good idea—but yellow walls can make people feel agitated. So think about sticking with a friendly shade and possibly avoiding its use in rooms where you spend the bulk of your time.

OPPOSITE PAGE Yellow this bright makes a striking accent, whereas it could be overbearing on all four walls.

ABOVE LEFT Yellow and white pillows pop right out of the scene on Lee Kleinhelter's shady porch.

TOP RIGHT Bolsters in yellow plaid give these curtained bunk beds an extra inviting appeal.

BOTTOM RIGHT Soft yellow walls can make almost any room feel warm and sunny.

TOP LEFT A red, white, and mustard scheme contributes to the retro charm of this bedroom.

BOTTOM LEFT It is possible to use yellow, red, and blue without creating a preschool effect. It all depends on the shades you choose.

BOTTOM RIGHT Yellow subway tiles warm up a bath.

OPPOSITE PAGE Bright yellow has a reflective quality that can make a space seem to glow.

Green

John Lum's favorite color is green, including the most intense and acid shades (see the island on page 168 for evidence). He sees it as healthful and easy to work with. And he's far from alone. Green is nearly always a popular choice, though certainly some shades are more popular than others. (Along with "harvest gold," avocado may never recover its reputation after the advent of '70s appliances in the hue.) Green is also popular with Michael Bell (check out his kitchen on page 110), who particularly loves green with blue. If anyone ever asks him about the combo's longevity, he says, "Look out the window—it's nature. It'll never go out of style." Blue and green are neighbors on the color wheel, which makes them naturally harmonious, but the nature point is a potent one. Green

is nature's neutral and, as such, the backdrop for literally every color under the sun. While some people might prefer certain pairings over others, it is rare to hear anyone suggest that any color clashes with green.

The famous exception to the easygoing green rule, though, is red—green's complement. The best way to combine them is to pick one of the two in its true shade, and the other off in one direction or another from its true hue. So perhaps choose apple, sage, or blue-green when using true red; and maybe red-orange or a pinkish berry-red when using true green. Beware of "hunter green" and burgundy, though—a combo that is to the '80s as avocado is to the '70s.

OPPOSITE PAGE The trick to using true green and true red in the same space is to use small doses and give them some distance.

ABOVE Light apple-green walls and even lighter toile pillows keep this wood-and-leather room from feeling too masculine.

TOP LEFT Grass-green cabinets and trim make for a distinctive kitchen.

TOP RIGHT Olive-green walls are a moody backdrop for multicolored quilts.

BOTTOM LEFT Earthy green upholstery combines beautifully with wood and stone.

BOTTOM RIGHT A bright yellow-green frame and blue-green containers perk up an austere bathroom.

OPPOSITE PAGE This charming bathroom brings the phrase "minty fresh" to mind.

Purple

OPPOSITE PAGE A series of purple towels on hooks serves almost as art on this bathroom wall.

TOP RIGHT Gray-grape walls are an elegant surprise in a home office.

BOTTOM RIGHT A deep-eggplant armchair adds richness to this den filled with tans and oranges.

P urple can be polarizing—people tend to either love it or hate it. But the fact that so few people use it is exactly what makes it appealing to Tia Zoldan, who likes the unexpected.

Representing the marriage of red and blue, purples range from red-violet to blue-violet; the redder a purple is, the warmer it is. True purple is associated with royalty and religion, while the paler shades (lilac and lavender) are largely the province of little girls. But that does not mean purple doesn't have a sophisticated side: deep shades like aubergine or eggplant can bring depth and drama to a space, especially when played off of a warm color like red or orange. Even the "little girl" shades can look elegant when paired with lots of rich browns. In Carl Palasota's home, which is full of subtleties (see pages 92–93), the doors and shutters are a purple so deep it appears black to anyone who isn't paying attention. He's paired it with an equally deceptive putty green.

As noted before, purple is yellow's complement but the two are rarely seen together indoors. If you're among the masses who love purple in the garden, against all that green, consider bringing exactly that combination indoors.

DESIGNER
TIA ZOLDAN ON

Purple for the Color-Shy

T ia Zoldan finds purple to be "great for people who are scared of color and tend to like rooms that are very neutral." That's because, like the deep eggplant of Carl Palasota's doors and shutters, it can go dark enough that it's barely perceived as a color, while still adding character to the room.

LEFT AND BELOW
You don't have to be a little girl to want a lavender bedroom. Chocolate brown makes it more grown up, whereas multiple shades and pops of other color keep it on the youthful side.

RIGHT What could make a bath more memorable than violet-stained concrete and an acid-yellow–tiled niche?

Orange

Famously, nothing rhymes with orange, but somehow everything goes with it. The only real hazard is black with orange, which inevitably evokes Halloween if there are no other colors in the mix. And when orange and its complement, blue, are used full strength, the result can be garish. But few things are lovelier than true orange paired with softer or grayer shades of blue; and the same goes for a brighter blue with a less vibrant orange. Orange is often used in combination with either of blue's next-door neighbors, blue-violet or blue-green. But Carl Palasota, who excels at neutral interiors, has been using an earthy shade of orange

quite a lot lately. He says, "I've found that [orange] to be a neutral." To him, it's a good, subtle way to inject a little something extra into a space.

When you say "blue" or "green" to a group of people, they're all likely to picture a different shade. Say "orange," and people picture more or less the same hue—the color of a perfectly ripened orange. There are times when that orange is the color of the moment, but it never really goes out of style. Variances of orange, though, tend to be overlooked or simply more subject to trends. From apricot and salmon to bright red-orange and the darkest rust, orange is more diverse than you might think.

OPPOSITE PAGE A coat of apricot paint amplifies the space above the mantel, a natural focal point, without overpowering the artwork hung upon it.

ABOVE An oversized, statement-making designer lamp in bright orange is softened by its neutral surroundings.

TOP LEFT A little bit of orange—here, in a bath mat and some towels—goes a long way toward enlivening a neutral space.

TOP RIGHT In Mexico, it's common to find a strong color used quite liberally, as in this indoor-outdoor room's orange on the ceiling, walls, and display niches.

BOTTOM Orange accessories in Lee Kleinhelter's living room play off the pale green sideboard in the hallway.

OPPOSITE PAGE As complements (that is, opposites on the color wheel), orange and blue are perfect foils to each other.

Pink

The magenta throw is a glamorous partner for this chaise set against gilded wall-paper and a satin shag rug.

Unlike the colors discussed up to this point, pink isn't technically a color family unto itself; not a primary, secondary, or even tertiary color, it is a subset of red. Add white to red and you get pink, its exact shade determined by what red you start with and how much white you add. But in a discussion of the major colors, pink earns its place.

There are cultures where pink doesn't carry the connotations it does in the United States. Legendary fashion editor Diana Vreeland famously called pink "the navy blue of India," and it's equally embraced in Mexico. But in the U.S., its appeal is less universal and more subject to fluctuations. In fashion—especially men's fashion—pink tends to be either the color of the moment or simply not worn. (In recent years, if J. Crew—known for its color choices and names—was making a garment in eight colors, five of them might be shades of pink. Now the pinks are few and farther between.) But for interiors, pink's usage falls to those who love it and always will, or, of course, to little girls' rooms, where it always reigns supreme. There, it's typically layered on in multiple shades and patterns. Ironically, a century ago pink was associated with little boys and light blue with little girls. It's hard to imagine that now, so deeply engrained are our associations.

Tia Zoldan is one who loves pink. While she says her favorite color "probably changes every six months," right now it's fuchsia. "It's rich but bright," she notes, "and such a feminine touch in a room. If there's a man living in the house, you kind of feel bad, but my husband doesn't care. He knows it'll change in six months."

TOP Light pink walls give this richly colored Parisian living room a rosy glow.

BOTTOM LEFT Mexican interiors are all about strong doses of the boldest colors, such as this hot-pink shelf and tablecloth, paired with red glass.

BOTTOM RIGHT This iconic midcentury-modern chair is a looker in lipstick pink.

DESIGNER
TIA ZOLDAN ON

Pink for Grown-Ups

Tia Zoldan says the key to using pink outside of a little girl's room is to use a high-impact shade in controlled amounts. "If you like pink," she says, "I wouldn't do all the walls in pink, just do a chair or even a bolster. And that says enough."

TOP LEFT For her daughter's room, Tia Zoldan used pink as an accent against pale shades of blue-green.

BOTTOM LEFT Lisa Rowe combined barely-pink walls and haute upholstery for an uncommonly elegant nursery.

BOTTOM RIGHT A button-tufted head-board, bright accents, and bubblegum pink on walls and ceiling make for a classic "princess" room.

OPPOSITE PAGE Raspberry bolsters and pink gingham look perfectly grown up when surrounded by sandy browns.

Brown

While the colors in the red-orange-yellow part of the color wheel are considered "hot" or "warm," the warmest color of all is brown. Brown is what you get when you stir together any two colors from across the wheel (making mud , essentially), and browns can have undertones of just about any other color—resulting in reddish browns, yellowish browns, and so on. The brown family ranges from the palest tan to the darkest chocolate, and, being neutral, brown goes with everything.

New York designer Robin Bell is another whose favorite colors change constantly, but when we spoke to her, during the Christmas season, she was under the spell of chestnuts. "I've got all of these glass vases of different shapes and I'm thinking of filling them all with chestnuts," she said. "But I'm now thinking of browns, and especially how they relate to mercury and greens."

Nearly every room benefits from some brown, and most rooms start out with at least a little, by virtue of containing wood elements—from floors to furnishings. Generally, the more brown you introduce into a room, the cozier it will feel. A popular trick with designers working on small spaces— a powder room or small bedroom—is to paint the entire space a very dark brown, making a virtue of the smallness by turning it into a cocoon.

Brown's best trait, though, may be its ability to take the edge off of very bright colors, providing a way for even the timid among us to use them. If you've got a room that's predominantly black and white and you add a vibrant color—say, orange— that color will be amplified. But place the same orange element in a room full of tan, straw, and brown, and the effect will be much softer.

OPPOSITE PAGE A light floor and white linens keep this chocolate-ceilinged cocoon of mixed browns from feeling overly dark.

ABOVE LEFT Medium-brown accents stand out against an all-white background.

TOP RIGHT A large, velvety-brown painting provides contrast for glossy white furnishings.

BOTTOM RIGHT Honey-colored wood floors, a brown blanket, and a café au lait accent wall warm up this sleek bedroom.

TOP LEFT Icy blue walls offer a cool backdrop for layers of brown burlap, plaid, and toile.

BOTTOM LEFT This bathroom is anything but chilly, thanks to lots of wood and a striking bronze tub.

RIGHT A wall of chocolate-painted built-ins tempers the bright yellow Chinese Chippendale chairs.

Gray

Warm gray walls frame this home office, tucked into an ivory-painted bay of windows.

White is the absence of color, and black is the culmination of all color. Add white to black and you get gray. Like browns, grays can tip toward any part of the color wheel, resulting in blue-grays, yellow-grays, and the like. Combining warm (brownish) and cool (bluish) grays in the same space can be challenging. But if you think about what happens to colors as you lighten them with white, they move closer and closer to pastel. A drop of black into the mix lends a slight gray-ness that makes nearly every color feel more sophisticated: mint green becomes sage, baby blue becomes slate, and so on. So even in choosing *colors*, that element of grayness can be important.

While most people think of tints of brown (beige, khaki, sand) when they hear the word *neutral*, the truest neutral is a perfectly balanced gray. Because it betrays no color of its own, it's the shade of gray on which artists and jewelers display their work, and also the color that's used as primer for paint jobs, from walls to cars. Gray primer neutralizes whatever it goes over and doesn't impact the color of whatever goes over it.

But gray is not just for primer anymore. In recent years, it's become extremely popular for interiors. Two of our experts, Carl Palasota and Lisa Rowe, cite it as their current favorite color. Palasota says he lives in shades of khaki, both in his home and his wardrobe, but finds himself increasingly drawn to gray. Rowe, too, loves the diversity of grays—from cool silvery tones to warmer brownish-grays. When there's a particular color or piece of artwork you want to show off, think like a jeweler and pair it with gray.

TOP LEFT Carl Palasota pairs subtly varied cool grays with a gray-brown ceiling.

TOP RIGHT Silvery-gray velvet plays off of warm wood.

BOTTOM For this layered, shades-of-gray scheme, even the wood floors and trim have been stained gray.

TOP LEFT A perfect neutral gray is unexpected on kitchen cabinets.

TOP RIGHT A gray-and-white painted floor sparks up an all-white bathroom.

BOTTOM LEFT Soft gray and white stripes strike a balance between formal and informal on this window seat.

BOTTOM RIGHT A rich gray highlights the form of this built-in bench, and sets off the saffron pillow.

OPPOSITE PAGE A gray wall and chrome legs break up a space filled with shades of honey brown.

There's an old decorating adage that says every room needs something black. That might mean anything from a weathered side table providing a bit of contrast, to an ebony floor grounding a lofty space, to ink-black walls setting off pale or colorful furnishings. As with white, finish matters: black lacquer or patent leather will make an entirely different impression than black suede or cotton. An easy trick for adding a note of interest to any room is to introduce an item in a black-and-white pattern—a zebra-print ottoman maybe, or an awning-striped bolster. Because black is as dramatic as it gets, even a little can go a long way.

OPPOSITE PAGE This setting is so artful, it's easy to miss that it's a kitchen. Black base cabinets contribute to that effect.

TOP LEFT A black-and-white floral pattern on the risers turns this stairwell into something special.

TOP RIGHT A black leather chair anchors a space composed of pale neutrals.

BOTTOM Button-tufted dining chairs in glossy black patent leather are undeniably dressy.

Chapter 3.

Using Neutrals

Only black and white can truly be called colorless, and yet when most people hear the term *neutral,* they think of pale tints of black and brown—soft colors like beige, gray, and taupe. As discussed in Chapter 2, some browns and grays are more neutral than others, while several "colors" partner so well with others that they, too, can reasonably be described as neutral. No matter how you define the term, neutrals have a fundamental role to play when it comes to choosing colors for a room.

For people with a strong feeling for color, the idea of a neutral space can seem boring. To others, nothing sounds more soothing. But neutrals have a role to play in nearly every room, no matter what the overall mix of colors. Even Tia Zoldan, who uses color liberally, advocates for building a room's palette on a neutral foundation. She says she likes to keep the floors, walls, and major upholstered pieces neutral, and then to add measured doses of color into the space—"especially in bigger rooms, and rooms the whole family uses a lot." She saves the "riskier" colors for smaller spaces—"rooms that aren't the family room."

Black, White, and Tan

Black and white, the ultimate complements, can make for a striking room all on their own. The importance of white and black elements in any room, though, is hard to overstate. Black provides depth and acts as a visual anchor, especially in a pale space. White, on the other hand, provides crispness and sets off other colors. Elements in light-brown shades like taupe or tan are to a room as khaki pants are to a wardrobe. They bring a softness—even casualness—that tones down whatever they're paired with. So brownish neutrals can keep very colorful elements in check, as can grays.

OPPOSITE PAGE Carl Palasota layered grays on top of the black and white in this small dressing room. The brown of the drum provides warm contrast, along with the wood floor inlays.

TOP RIGHT Panels of laminate in black, gray, and birch create an artful grid on these kitchen cabinets.

BOTTOM RIGHT Brown walls in a bedroom create a cozy environment and set off white bed linens.

Beyond the White Box

Some think of all-neutral spaces as calming, others dismiss them as bland or drab, and some even consider a reliance on neutrals to be a cop-out. But our Design Panel agreed that creating a successful neutral space—that is to say, an *interesting* neutral space—is at least as challenging as creating a successful color-filled one.

How does one get from the boring white box to an intriguingly neutral space? As in any room, a mix of textures and colors is key. Even if your "colors" are black, white, khaki, and walnut, that affords plenty of opportunity for contrast. If, on the other hand, you're keeping the number of colors to a minimum, make sure to vary the texture and finish so the parts don't all blur into each other. If you're planning an all-beige bathroom, for example, think about a limestone floor and countertop, matte-painted walls, and a glazed-ceramic–tile backsplash. And never underestimate the power of pattern, especially in a neutral setting. Providing a lot of visual interest and contrast, however subtle, is what brings a neutral space to life. As Carl Palasota says, it's about "really discovering how intense neutrals can be."

CLOCKWISE FROM TOP LEFT Although this bathroom is strictly black and white, there's a lot of visual interest—from the ebonized cabinetry to the geometric fields of off-black tile.

Set against white walls and a strong mix of wood tones and leather, variously colored and patterned accents don't alter the overall neutral flavor of this home.

A boldly patterned wallpaper feels toned down when done in neutral shades. This glamorous paper is paired with raw wood for stylistic contrast.

Using a very narrow range of colors can create a serene setting; variations in shade and pattern keep it interesting.

A taupe sofa matches the ceiling's weathered planks, and the black trunk echoes the front door. The windowpane check feels slightly whimsical on the wooden wingback chair.

DESIGNER
MICHAEL BELL ON

Texture and Neutrals

When asked about the challenges a neutral room presents, Michael Bell cut to the chase: "My unwritten rule: the more neutral a space is, the more you need to look at texture to make it interesting." For his Maine cottage (pages 86–87), he used sisal, wood, and glass to create textural contrast in his white rooms.

Intrinsic Color

This bathroom has color and texture to spare, thanks to variegated slate walls, a warm wood vanity, and a floor of large ivory tiles inlaid with stripes of patterned metal.

Essentially all rooms contain materials that were colored by Mother Nature and that, used thoughtfully, can contribute greatly to any look you're trying to achieve. It's entirely acceptable to mix various stones, woods, metals, or fibers within a space, but you do want to consider the coloration of these elements and how they relate to the whole.

Brick, Stone, and Tile

Clay and stone are wide-ranging in form and color, and tile is even more so. Picture slate, brick, and limestone, and you've got three very different colors—variegated gray, deep red, and a golden beige, respectively—and that's just scratching the surface. Granites and marbles come in a surprising array of colors. But the surface character of each of these materials also contributes to the tone it sets. For instance, polished white marble is cool (both visually and to the touch), while terra-cotta is much warmer, and cleft slate has its own unique texture.

DESIGNER
ROBIN BELL ON

Permanence

"My advice about woods, marbles, et cetera," says Robin Bell, thinking of a friend who put expensive blue granite counters in her kitchen, "is don't be bold with those, because they're often used with permanence." She compares it to wanting a pink diamond in an engagement ring: "You better be sure you're going to love that pink diamond for a very, very long time.

"For the bones [of a room]—the stones, the woods—stick with things that are easy to live with, and bring on the colors in places that are easier to change."

ABOVE A wall of classic chalkboard surface and the battered gray door from a safe give this kitchen extra character.

RIGHT Exposed red-brick walls bring inherent warmth to any space.

BELOW LEFT Tile comes in a vast array of naturally colored materials, including these cork penny tiles.

BELOW RIGHT Terra-cotta, a color and material closely associated with gardens, helps tie this room to the outdoors.

Wood and Fiber

There are inherent differences from one wood or natural fiber (jute, hemp, sisal, rattan) to the next. Unfinished pine and unfinished cherry, for example, are two very different colors. Then there's the issue of stains and sealers, which draw further distinctions and can even alter the inherent color entirely. Consider, too, the difference between a floor crafted of salvaged barn siding, weathered to a soft gray, and one made of freshly milled and highly polished walnut—the effect is decidedly different. So when choosing and combining woods or natural fibers, look at them in terms of not just light or dark but also the comparative colorations: one material might look quite yellow, pink, or orange next to another.

Metal

Most household metals break down into two classes: silver-tone (gray) metals, such as steel, zinc, chrome, and nickel; and gold-tone (yellow) metals, the most common of which is brass. (Copper, not seen much in interiors, is pink by comparison.) And metal is another case where finish matters: aged brass gives a different effect than polished brass; brushed nickel has a much warmer look than chrome.

Metal factors into rooms in the form of hardware—hinges, pulls, light fixtures—and furnishings. Too much of any one metal—say, a room where the chair legs, tables, and lamps are all chrome—can feel monotonous and overly matched, but many people are timid about mixing. Again, it is fine to mix your metals, as long as you're considering their colors and how they relate in the space.

TOP LEFT A variety of wickers and woods creates a lot of color in a space, accented by blue-green glass.

TOP RIGHT Wood is the perfect complement for marble's chilly nature.

BOTTOM LEFT For this tableau, silver and gold tones are married with great effect, set off by the dark wood table.

BOTTOM CENTER Sisal flooring, a jute basket, and a blackened-tin table bring color and textural contrast to this bedroom.

BOTTOM RIGHT Even among the silver-tone metals, there is variation in color.

Whitening Up

THIS PAGE A watery blue floor topped with a textural area rug sets off white furnishings in a mix of finishes. The brown leather ottoman is an unexpected note of contrast.

OPPOSITE PAGE The reflectiveness of the floor, Lucite chairs, and glass tabletop helped Michael Bell achieve the ethereal quality he was looking for.

W hen Michael Bell and his partner bought this Maine cottage—a weekend escape from Washington, DC—it had dark-brown paneling on all the walls and ceilings. "It was like a cave," he says. "Up there, they laughed at us. They say everyone who lives south of Boston paints everything white, and everyone from north of Boston keeps the dark." But for Bell, it was a no-brainer: he wanted it light and bright.

The Elements

- **Walls and Ceiling:** White-painted paneling

- **Floors:** Hardwood painted pale, glossy blue, with natural-fiber rugs

- **Furnishings:** White cotton sofa, pillows, and armchair; white-painted side chairs, end tables, and coffee tables; Lucite dining chairs at glass-topped table; brown leather ottoman

- **Window Coverings:** White wood blinds

- **Accents:** Unfinished wood table lamps; brushed-nickel reading lamp; wicker basket of throws

Shades of Sand

THIS PAGE Striped pillows play off the contrasting shades of brown in all the wood, rattan, and upholstery.

OPPOSITE PAGE, TOP The light-colored, open-frame arm-chairs in front of this fireplace have an endless-summer feeling about them.

OPPOSITE PAGE, BOTTOM White roller shades disappear when retracted, inviting the green of the garden into the space.

In this Hamptons summer home, sunlight is maximized with white walls and ceilings and lots of windows. But an added measure of warmth comes from the multi-textured, shades-of-tan furnishings. Two seating areas are made up of three different takes on rattan, that summer classic: dark-wood frames with open-weave rattan backs and wrapped arms; boxy frames covered in smooth, woven rattan; and more traditional rattan armchairs paired with rattan globe floor lamps—all providing natural color and texture. In this setting, the jute rug mimics the nearby beach. Striped pillows spice things up just a touch, while the light fixtures and photographs nod subtly at the beach motif.

The Elements

- **Walls and Ceiling:** White-painted paneling

- **Floors:** Warm brown hardwood under jute rugs

- **Furnishings:** Wood and woven rattan seating, with tan upholstery; wood-and-glass coffee table; wood armoire and chest

- **Window Coverings:** White roller blinds

- **Accents:** Multibrown striped pillows; rattan globe floor lamps; life-preserver–inspired light fixtures; vintage black-and-white surfing and rowing photos

Material Riches

THIS PAGE This salvaged cable spool—a golden match for the exposed beams—was topped with zinc and paired with classic fiberglass chairs in white.

OPPOSITE PAGE, TOP AND BOTTOM The exposed steel support beams and rafters create geometry in the open space, as does the grid of white subway tile with its dark grout.

The owners of this home wanted it to have an open, industrial flavor, and that's precisely what they got. Plain white walls and bare windows form a backdrop for a host of utilitarian materials and surfaces, from the concrete floors to the exposed rafters and beams, with lots of steel, fiberglass, chrome, and subway tile in between. Sticking to the neutral palette allowed a large number of materials and surfaces to be combined successfully in the space—showing off their various assets without becoming busy.

The Elements

- **Walls:** Painted white

- **Ceiling:** White with exposed steel rafters and wood beams

- **Floors:** Poured concrete foundation left exposed

- **Countertops:** Concrete

- **Backsplash:** White subway tiles with dark grout

- **Cabinets:** Ebonized wood with chrome pulls; island with backlit translucent panels

- **Appliances:** Commercial-style stainless steel

- **Furnishings:** Taupe upholstered sectional; white fiberglass Eames chairs with zinc-topped spool table; vintage steel sideboard; rusted tractor seat barstools

- **Window Coverings:** None

- **Accents:** Refinished vintage street lights hung above the island

Deceptively Neutral

THIS PAGE The boxy white fireplace provides contrast to the mottled plaster walls. A checkerboard enlivens any room.

OPPOSITE PAGE, CLOCKWISE FROM TOP On white-painted pieces, black edging highlights the shapes.

The half-doors and shutters throughout the house appear to be black, but are actually a deep shade of purple.

Black-and-white chairs stand out against the soft backdrop. The trim on the walls and doors is a subtle gray-green.

If anyone knows what it takes to make a neutral space vibrant and intriguing, it's Carl Palasota. For his own Louisiana home, he started with the plaster walls, which were inspired by the color of antique French terra-cotta urns common to the area. Next came the white checkerboard painted onto the wood floors, plus gray-green trim and deep-purple shutters that appear, respectively, putty and black at first, and reveal their true colors slowly. (The trim color was inspired by a piece of Hermès leather; Palasota had paint custom-mixed to match the shade.) A geometric white fireplace completes the structural picture. Into this mix, Palasota introduced furnishings in an eclectic assortment of styles, colors, finishes, and fabrics—ranging from black to white, from velvet to gingham to a barely-there paisley. The result is the furthest thing from plain. (See also the sleeping porch on page 77.)

The Elements

- **Walls and Ceiling:** Hand-troweled plaster the color of aged terra-cotta

- **Floors:** Salvaged barn decking, painted with white checkerboard in main room

- **Furnishings:** Chairs, daybeds, and settees in white, black, and a mix of wood tones

- **Window Coverings:** Deep-eggplant shutters and variously patterned curtains

- **Accents:** Throw pillows in several neutral shades; the urn that inspired the wall color; turtle shells and other idiosyncratic objects; drums used as accent tables

Room for Repose

THIS PAGE Gray bedding combines with the brown bed and floor to create a restful setting.

OPPOSITE PAGE, TOP AND BOTTOM The broad gray stripe is used as a minor accent on a bed pillow and a more substantial accent on a loveseat.

This gray, white, and wood bedroom might have been a bit drab if not for the introduction of an elegant slate-gray striped fabric to complement the narrower gray stripe of the pillowcases. Covering an accent pillow and a loveseat (which has been quirkily joined to a pair of ornate bases), the broad stripes create interest in the room without upsetting the restful mood. Two sets of paintings of nighttime seascapes contribute to that, the moody blues playing nicely off the grays. A giant red pot (holding a stately palm) provides exactly the right note of contrast.

The Elements

- **Walls:** White-painted beadboard

- **Ceiling:** Glossy white-painted wood boards and rafters

- **Floors:** Weathered hardwood planks

- **Furnishings:** Dark-wood platform bed with built-in nightstands; gray-striped loveseat

- **Window Coverings:** White floor-length curtains; wood blinds

- **Accents:** Heather-gray duvet; charcoal wool blanket; pillows and upholstery in a mix of gray stripes; nighttime seascape paintings; shell-encrusted lamps; palm in dark-red glazed pot

Chapter 4

Keeping It Simple

Color doesn't have to be complicated, or even a big commitment. The simple approach might mean using only small, easily changed bursts of color, or it might mean picking a single color but using it liberally. In this chapter, we explore those ideas as well as ways to narrow down the color wheel to a more approachable wedge from which to work. As you'll see, simple isn't necessarily synonymous with subtle—you can arrive at even the most vibrant rooms through simple paths.

The Minimalist Approach

Bringing color into a room does not have to mean giving up your white walls and neutral furnishings. It needn't even mean picking up a paintbrush. Minimalists, take heart: there are lots of low-key, high-impact ways to incorporate color.

Art and Objects

While there are those who strive for a truly color-free room (and some who accomplish it), for most of us the only way to achieve that objective is to not put anything in the space. At least, not any of the stuff that makes us who we are. The fact is, a lot of household color is intrinsic—and not just in the sense of woods and metals, as discussed in Chapter 3. If you bring a houseplant into a room,

for example, you've added green. Hang a painting or photograph on the wall, and you've contributed its colors to the space.

Then there is the matter of objects and collections. Decorators have been known to balk at the riot of colors a wall of books represents, but book-lovers count on that very tapestry of spines to bring a room to life. If you have a tribal headdress from Africa or a set of lacquered boxes from China, that may be all the color your living room needs. Likewise, if you collect colored dishes or glassware of one sort or another, storing it on open shelves in an otherwise neutral kitchen not only adds color to the room but also ensures that your collection gets the attention it deserves.

OPPOSITE PAGE
Even a purely white room becomes colorful when a wall of books is involved.

ABOVE LEFT A colorful collection of vintage boxes brightens a blank stairwell.

TOP RIGHT A bright piece of art may be all the color you need.

BOTTOM RIGHT Displayed in (and on) a glass-fronted case, collections of dishware and blown glass show off their colors.

Small Furniture and Accessories

"I personally don't like to designate rooms with paint colors," says Lee Kleinhelter. "I like to have a blank palette and express color through fabrics and accessories—lamps, rugs, pillows. It's a way to experiment and push the envelope with something that can be easily removed." Designers Tia Zoldan and Charles De Lisle also tend toward a neutral backdrop, and both like to bring in color with the furnishings. De Lisle might modulate the shade of his neutral from the ceiling to the walls to the trim, but then, he says, "I usually insert a hot color or a more saturated color in the furniture." Zoldan finds that if you've got a colorful painting and even a single small chair in a vibrant color, "when you walk into the room and you see that, you think *oh that's so beautiful and colorful*, and you get the impression that there's a lot of color in the room, but there's not." Of course, the larger the item in question, the larger the commitment; an orange sofa will make a bigger statement than orange throw pillows, but it'll also cost you more and be harder to replace. As Kleinhelter suggests, the easier it is to swap out an item—a rug, for instance, or a small footstool—the more daring you might find yourself.

TOP LEFT Colorful fabric turns a simple upholstered headboard into a conversation piece.

TOP CENTER Who says color has to go on the walls? Here, a collection of rugs does the trick.

TOP RIGHT Keeping color to something as simple to change as throw pillows allows for bold combinations.

BOTTOM LEFT A single red pillow picks up on the pair of lacquered chairs, while the chair seats and additional pillows echo the front door.

BOTTOM CENTER Painting a wooden dining table is a simple task that can make a big difference.

BOTTOM RIGHT A desk upholstered in bright red, with brass nailheads, would brighten up anyone's workday. Blue accents add to its appeal.

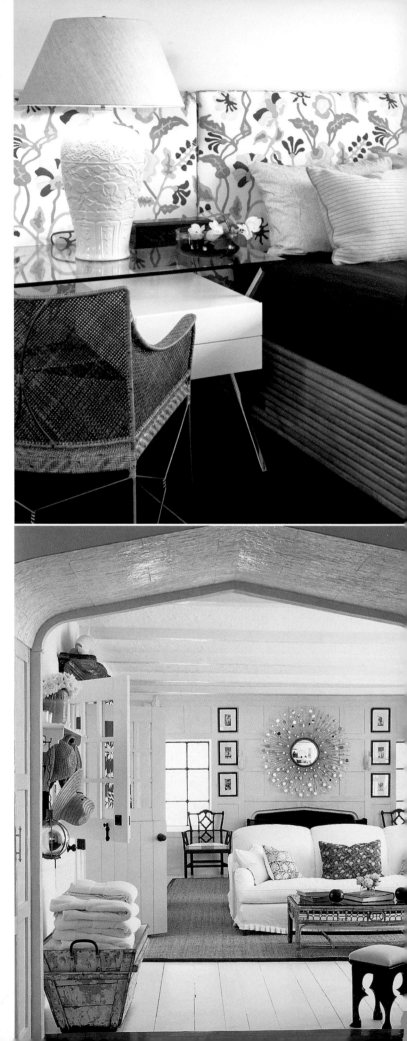

Contrast Trim

Painting walls a color and trim white is standard operating procedure—why not change things up and do the opposite? Colored trim not only calls attention to beautiful millwork around windows and doors but also, in the process, it can draw attention to a nice view out those windows, literally framing the view. For instance, if you've got windows that look out on a garden and are not in need of window coverings, trimming them in a beautiful color is a great way to make the most of that asset.

Accent Walls

An accent wall generally feels like a smaller commitment than painting all four walls, and also allows you to use a bolder color because there will be less of it. An accent wall can be a good way to create interest in an architecturally undistinguished space, to draw attention through a sequence of spaces, or to anchor a large piece of furniture in a space. It isn't necessary in all cases even to paint the whole wall—an enormous rectangle of color behind a bed or couch can stand in for artwork or a headboard.

ABOVE Whether the room is country or formal, bright or subtle, traditional or contemporary, colored paint on the trim of windows and doors boosts character.

OPPOSITE PAGE A large, painted rectangle in a matching shade anchors the pink couch in this neutral space.

Monochromatic Schemes

Perhaps the very simplest of all approaches to color is the monochrome approach—picking just one single color to incorporate into a space. The effect of the color can range from subtle to striking, depending on how you deploy it.

One Right Hue

The first step toward a monochromatic scheme, of course, is picking your color. If you have a favorite, have loved it forever, and expect to continue loving it for years to come, then you're already halfway there. If you're searching for the right color, on the other hand, ask yourself what you want to achieve. Do you want the room to feel warm or cool? Bold or serene? Looking through the color profiles in Chapter 2 will help you understand the effect any given color will have on a space.

How Much Is Enough

Step two, then, is deciding how to use that color, and in what quantity. Say you've chosen a golden yellow. You might paint all four walls that shade and keep all of your furnishings neutral. Or you might take Lee Kleinhelter's favorite route. She feels you create "a cleaner feel" when you keep the walls white and repeat a single color throughout a space in various forms. For instance, your lamp, rug pattern, and throw pillows might all be in your chosen yellow. "I think it's nice when things are in layers and matching," she says.

Keep in mind that the more you use of a bold color, the bolder the room will feel. In other words, the same lime green will feel bolder used on all four walls than scattered around the space in smaller doses. And the opposite is also true: very small doses of a subtle color may wind up feeling even subtler than you are aiming for. So when making your selection, it is important to factor the distribution of the color into the question of what that color will be.

DESIGNER
ROBIN BELL ON

Colored Walls

Robin Bell counsels people to keep art in mind when painting walls a color: "Very often people pick their favorite color, and it's a very pretty color, and they want it to be on the wall. The problem with pretty colors is they often fight with everything else going onto the wall. If you like a color, pick its slightly drabber sister because it will better highlight the art you place on those walls." Or make the walls neutral and use your chosen color in other ways.

OPPOSITE PAGE AND THIS PAGE, TOP Cobalt blue makes a different impression when used in large fields of glossy tile versus soft cotton patterns and botanical prints.

BOTTOM LEFT A punchy red from the hallway repeats on open kitchen shelves. The abundant wood counterbalances the brightness of the red.

BOTTOM RIGHT Bubblegum pink repeats in the geometric-patterned headboard and bed skirt, floral pillows, wide borders on the duvet and shams, and a matching storage bin.

Varying the Tone

The third thing to consider with a monochromatic scheme is whether you want to limit yourself to one precise shade or use tonal variations thereof. Whereas using a single shade creates a crisp, clean look, variation gives a space more depth of character. John Lum finds himself taking this approach a lot these days. "I'm starting to be more limited in my color sense," he says, "trying to come up with more complex schemes." What he means by *complex* isn't "throwing in a lot of different colors," but rather "trying to limit the variations to tone and value, for a more sophisticated effect."

TOP LEFT This soft green appears even softer when the tone varies from one tile to the next.

BOTTOM LEFT Bright peacock blue is made more interesting by the modulation of the color, both in the colored panels on the wall and in the rug.

TOP RIGHT This bed and bath offer the best of both approaches: the serenity of a single shade of orange in the bedroom; a livelier mix of oranges in the bath.

BOTTOM RIGHT When using shades of a color, like these blues, it doesn't feel like a big stretch to throw in a multihued pattern based on that color.

OPPOSITE PAGE A single pale blue is used lavishly on the walls and window seat, partnered with a bolder blue in a bigger pattern.

A nalogous colors are those that sit side by side on the color wheel. Because they're from the same part of the spectrum, they have shared characteristics that make them naturally harmonious. As such, they offer a simple way to narrow down your color choices.

Which Hues and How Many

If we think of the color wheel as the color *pie*, a mono-chromatic scheme would be just a tiny sliver of a pie piece (containing a single color and its lighter and darker shades). An analogous scheme would be more of a wedge. What matters in choosing your wedge is which part of the pie you slice from, and how big of a piece you cut.

Remember that half of the color wheel is made up of cool colors (yellow-green through violet) and the other half of warm colors (red-violet through yellow). Taking colors from only the cool side will net you a cool room, for example. But it's possible to take a slice that includes some warmer and cooler shades. Rather than using red, orange, and yellow, for instance, try orange, yellow, and green. Blue and violet, both cool, will create a different effect than violet and red, a cool and a hot.

How wide you make your slice is entirely up to you. You might choose to use just two colors—yellow and green, perhaps, or red and orange. For a little more depth of color, you might stick to two colors, say blue and green, but use multiple shades of the two (perhaps several blues and a couple of greens). Or you might choose to cut your slice wider, maybe even using the entire cool side of the wheel, or the entire warm side. The more colors (and shades of those colors) you use, the more complex your palette will become, even while limiting yourself to just a portion of the wheel.

OPPOSITE PAGE Green and blue-green are natural companions, especially in similar values. The patterned pillow maintains the tone while adding interest.

TOP RIGHT Red, orange, and yellow—the very hottest colors—make this patio feel like it's south of the border.

BOTTOM RIGHT Even a small dose of green (here, in a tropical print) cools down its neighbors, yellow and orange.

OPPOSITE PAGE
Michael Bell chose a light apple-green for the cabinets in his cottage kitchen. Powder-blue small appliances echo the floor color, and the rug repeats the combo.

TOP LEFT Colors that bump up against each other in the spectrum, as blue and purple do, make easy companions in any room.

TOP RIGHT John Lum chose this lively tile in multiple blues and greens, then matched it to lime-green floor tiles and countertop.

BOTTOM LEFT A rug in soft shades of blue, green, and yellow is topped with a brighter yellow chair.

BOTTOM RIGHT Charles De Lisle is attracted to brightly colored tile patterns, which often come in analogous schemes like this one using shades of red and red-orange.

Collecting a Color

THIS PAGE Among all the black furnishings, a single chair is upholstered in the chosen blue.

OPPOSITE PAGE, LEFT A glass cabinet displays the collection. The warm brown floor and softly patterned rug keep the space from feeling stark.

OPPOSITE PAGE, RIGHT The barely-there painting and zebra-clad bench add complexity to the space while leaving the spotlight on the blues.

The owner of this home, as you may have already noticed, has a penchant for cerulean blue—so much so that she collects glassware, lamps, and vessels in the hue, both in ceramic and glass. If you've built an entire collection around a single brilliant color, why not build your room around that collection? Simply let the collection be the room's source of color. For this collector, that approach led to white walls and black furniture, along with pale, neutral artwork and a subtly patterned rug. A glass-fronted case (painted black, of course) displays the bulk of the blue wares, while others are scattered around the room. The black unifies a collection of furnishings in disparate styles. And to put an exclamation point on it all, an antique chair is upholstered in leather of the precise shade of blue.

The Elements

- **Walls and Ceiling:** White-painted wood planks and rafters

- **Floors:** Wood planks with a white-painted border and faded blue-and-brown rug

- **Furnishings:** New and vintage pieces in a mix of styles, all stained or painted black; chair at desk upholstered in blue leather; armchair in black leather; bench in zebra hide

- **Accents:** Lamp, vases and other collectibles in cerulean blue; white bed linens; brown-and-white throw

California Glow

THIS PAGE Robin Bell chose all-neutral furnishings to help her client feel more comfortable with colored walls.

OPPOSITE PAGE Layers of tinted glaze over paint give walls a character similar to Venetian plaster, minus the expense.

When Robin Bell first saw the sun-filled, neo-Spanish home she'd be redoing for a young client in Los Angeles, it was painted "the color of spoiled cream," which did nothing to enhance the beautiful plaster ceiling, corbels, and mantel. "Immediately when I looked at it," she says, "I thought of this marigold color." The client had bought a Spanish-style twisted walnut coffee table, her first "grown-up" piece of furniture, and wanted an equally grown-up space to put it in. But combined with the idea of the new furniture, the marigold walls felt a bit out of her comfort zone. To make the whole thing more approachable, Bell kept the furnishings entirely neutral. Giving the yellow extra depth, she had layers of glaze with additional pigment applied over the flat wall color. And to create plenty of interest with the neutral elements, she incorporated lots of different textures and finishes—including burnished wood, antiqued leather, and woven straw.

The Elements

- **Walls:** Yellow with layers of tinted glaze
- **Ceiling:** Off-white plaster
- **Floors:** Hardwood
- **Furnishings:** White sofa; brown leather armchair and ottoman; walnut coffee table; woven straw side table; antique armoire and chest of drawers; wood dining table; rattan dining chairs with woven seats and backs
- **Accents:** Botanical-print pillows; wood-framed mirrors; white ceramic table lamp; hand-colored 19th-century prints; aubergine glassware

Asymmetrically Green

THIS PAGE The wall on the living-room side of the loft is painted a subtle gray-green, which repeats in the rug.

OPPOSITE PAGE, TOP The two green walls extend past the black cabinets and minimalist gray kitchen into the twin bedrooms.

OPPOSITE PAGE, BOTTOM The wall along the stairs (by which the loft is accessed) is the livelier shade of green.

John Lum's favorite color is green, and in his San Francisco loft he used it in a way that is both liberal and subtle. The narrow space is lit by skylights and by windows at both ends—that is, along the shorter walls at the front and rear, both of which are painted white. The two walls that run the length of the space, however, were painted opposing shades of green, one so subtle as to be almost gray, the other the color of a ripe pear. Furnishings are kept entirely neutral, and an industrial-style kitchen at the center of the space, with a gray stucco wall, is flanked by rows of regimented black storage cabinets separated by white spacers. That march of black and white draws your attention down the twin hallways to the bedrooms, where the green walls pick back up again. Where using the same green on both walls might have made the symmetry of the space feel oppressive, the mismatched shades throw things off just enough to establish a more complex mood.

The Elements

- **Walls:** White, gray-green, pear green, and mottled gray

- **Ceiling:** Whitewashed rafters

- **Floors:** Douglas fir

- **Countertops:** White marble and black granite

- **Cabinets:** Blond-wood base cabinets; black ceiling-high storage cabinets

- **Furnishings:** Charcoal-gray sofa; off-white armchair; black-and-white modular coffee table; black Asian side chairs; carved wood stools; black barstools; weathered-wood Asian tripod stools

- **Window Coverings:** None

- **Accents:** Black-and-white artwork; blue-and-green striped rug; mismatched throw pillows; chrome task lamp; assorted Asian artifacts, including large wood Foo dog; vintage radio and clock collection; vintage metal canisters; vintage globes; architectural models

Playing Off Nature

THIS PAGE AND OPPOSITE PAGE, TOP Bright poppy-inspired hues stand out against the grays and woods around them, just like the flowers themselves.

OPPOSITE PAGE, BOTTOM The bright-against-wood effect is the same indoors and out.

Everything about this Northern California home is a tribute to the landscape in which it's built. This means lots of rugged materials and plenty of big windows for taking in the wind-swept meadows and ocean beyond. The aesthetic is spare and no-nonsense—Zen meets midcentury modern—but against the neutral backdrop of wood, concrete, and dark-gray fabrics, the homeowners arranged molded plastic armchairs in a bright pinkish-red, and amassed an assortment of throw pillows in countless shades of red, pink, orange, and yellow— some patterned, some solid. The effect is like another trademark of the landscape: the profusion of California poppies that blanket the area every spring.

The Elements

- **Walls and Ceilings:** Douglas fir

- **Floors:** Concrete

- **Furnishings:** Built-in benches with gray cushions; dining table in matching wood; poppy-colored molded plastic armchairs; gray and chrome chair with matching foot-stool; vintage Alvar Aalto rolling cart

- **Window Coverings:** None

- **Accents:** Gray patterned rug; suspended Eames sculpture; copious throw pillows in red, pink, orange, and yellow

Case Study

History Repeating

THIS PAGE The retro green combines with bin pulls and a farmhouse sink to give the kitchen an old-fashioned air.

OPPOSITE PAGE Wood rafters, white walls, cork floors, and kelly-green chairs all complement the light-green cabinets.

W ho says kitchen cabinets have to be neutral? Sure, in the event of a change of heart, repainting them is a bigger chore than repainting the walls, but when you pick smartly, it's worth it. This family knew they'd be spending a lot of time in their combination eat-in kitchen and laundry room, so they wanted it to feel cheerful and friendly. Warm-toned and soft underfoot, cork floors were a smart first choice. And then came cabinets in that classic midcentury laboratory green (revived almost single-handedly by Martha Stewart, who can't get enough of this color). With white walls, a vintage white enamel stove, and stainless-steel appliances, the space makes the most of the daylight. Kelly-green chairs at the simple wood table play off the shade of the cabinets.

The Elements

- **Walls:** White-painted beadboard

- **Ceiling:** White with wood rafters

- **Floors:** Cork

- **Countertops:** Wood

- **Cabinets:** Green-painted frame-and-panel

- **Appliances:** White vintage stove; stainless-steel hood, dishwasher drawers, and refrigerator

- **Furnishings:** Plain wooden dining table with kelly-green–painted chairs

- **Window Coverings:** None

- **Accents:** Aluminum industrial lights; white porcelain farmhouse sink; green patterned tablecloth

Eclectic Company

THIS PAGE AND OPPOSITE PAGE, BOTTOM LEFT A quirky mix of greens shows just how engaging mismatched colors can be.

OPPOSITE PAGE, TOP AND BOTTOM RIGHT De Lisle designed the dining table and customized the sideboard—laminating the former in blue Formica and the latter in his own black-and-white photograph. The photo above the sideboard adds another note of green.

When Charles De Lisle was hired to redo this midcentury home, originally designed by architect William Wurster, he adopted the architect's eclectic, anything-goes way with the interiors. It's an aesthetic that comes naturally to De Lisle—especially when it's a matter of color. "I like using color that doesn't match sometimes," he says. "Actually, all the time." Generally inclined to work with two or three colors in a given space, he's not shy about mixing in unpredictable shades of those colors, as with the off mix of blues and greens in this living and dining room. The daybed is a soft slate blue, for instance, while the dining table is aquamarine. The sofa in a slightly drab green is topped with twinkly emerald-green pillows and sits across the room from an armchair in chartreuse. It's a testament to just how loose you can be when you're working with analogous hues, thanks to their natural camaraderie.

The Elements

- **Walls:** White-painted adobe

- **Ceiling:** Wood with exposed rafters

- **Floors:** Concrete

- **Furnishings:** Midcentury modern armless sofa (upholstered in green), daybed (in blue), high-backed chair (in chartreuse) and dining chairs (in tan leather); black contemporary armchairs with tan leather upholstery; brass and stone coffee table; side tables in ebony and Lucite; dining table with blue Formica surfaces and exposed edges; sideboard with photo-laminated front

- **Accents:** Assorted paintings and photographs; neutral rug with geometric pattern; custom brass and rope "chandelier"; steel table lamp; brushed-aluminum floor lamp; emerald-green throw pillows

Blue Belle

THIS PAGE The breakfast room has blue trim and ceilings, along with blue-painted chairs covered in a blue-and-brown print. In the dining room beyond, it's blue walls with white trim, and a brown print on wood chairs.

OPPOSITE PAGE, TOP AND BOTTOM Blue walls, white trim, and sisal rugs are the backdrop to a wide variety of prints throughout the house.

This charming Southern cottage epitomizes the notion that simple doesn't mean simplistic. The homeowner decorated the entire house in just light blue and neutrals, but the way she varied the application from room to room is nothing short of inspired. First, the blue and white paints shift around from walls to trim to ceiling to the wood of some of the furnishings. Second, she's created her own surfaces in some cases, such as the papier-mâché walls in the breakfast nook and the oyster-shell–encrusted fireplace in the living room. Third, and quite importantly, there is no shortage of patterns: stripes, plaids, and florals; large- and small-scale; in blue, brown, or blue and brown. Some of the patterns repeat in various rooms, as do the sisal rugs that provide a common thread to it all. As a result, instead of the house seeming monotonous—the potential hazard of a monochromatic scheme—each room manages to have its own take on the concept. (See also the bedroom on page 68.)

The Elements

- **Walls:** Blue with white trim or vice versa

- **Ceiling:** Blue or white

- **Floors:** Hardwood with sisal rugs

- **Furnishings:** Wood dining chairs (painted, in the breakfast nook) with upholstered seats and backs; wood dining table; bamboo breakfast table with white-painted wicker base; window seat with blue-striped cushion; blue-striped roll-arm sofa; khaki-upholstered wingback chairs; antique wood coffee table; twin beds with bamboo headboards

- **Window Coverings:** Floor-length drapes in brown-and-blue floral; matchstick blinds

- **Accents:** Vintage chandeliers and sconces; throw pillows in a variety of blue and/or brown patterns; bedding and draped canopies in matching printed cotton

Simply Dynamic

THIS PAGE AND OPPOSITE PAGE A room full of neutral furnishings is utterly transformed when the walls are clad in a striking pattern.

A simple color solution doesn't automatically preclude a statement-making room, as seen in this Charles De Lisle–designed study. There's nothing complicated about a brown couch, wood table and file cabinets, white chairs, and steel work surfaces. Where this room gets its exuberant color is from one single decision: to upholster the walls in a bold botanical print. In the case of this one, it's a custom pattern De Lisle created (from leaves collected on the property and photocopied) and had printed on hemp. But there are countless beautiful wallpapers readily available these days. All it takes is the courage to use one. Pair it with neutral furnishings, as De Lisle did, and you're done.

The Elements

- **Walls:** Upholstered in custom-printed hemp
- **Ceiling:** Wood with exposed rafters
- **Floors:** Concrete, topped with neutral rug
- **Furnishings:** Chocolate-brown sofa; wood coffee table; wood filing cabinets with white tops; white and chrome desk chairs; rail-hung steel shelves and work surfaces

Stone and Sky

THIS PAGE Set among so many warm tones, the cool blue cherry-blossom mural is a standout.

OPPOSITE PAGE, TOP Glass tiles in the same blue as the mural give the effect of a waterfall.

OPPOSITE PAGE, BOTTOM Dark-wood cabinets contribute to the overall warm feel of the room.

The rocky terrain and ocean waters near this coastal California home were the inspiration for the master bathroom's palette of colors and materials, which combines rock and sandstone with watery blue tiles for tonal and textural contrast. The focal point of the room is the expanse of blue tile on the shower wall, painted with a mural of a cherry tree in bloom. Opposite the shower is a tub clad in rock, with a trompe l'oeil waterfall in the form of blue glass tile, laid vertically to further the effect. Large brown "leather" floor tiles, small sandstone shower-floor tiles, and the dark-wood veneer of the cabinetry combine with the gray-brown rock and the wood window frames for a host of warm tones to offset the cool blues.

The Elements

- **Walls:** Painted off-white; shower wall is sandstone bordering a blue tile mural; bath backsplash/wall is Eldorado stone veneer, running vertically, with inlay of blue glass tile, also running vertically

- **Ceiling:** Painted white

- **Floors:** Brown, leather-look porcelain tiles with glass-pebble inlay; sandstone tile in the shower

- **Countertops:** Dark-green marble

- **Cabinets:** African hardwood veneer

- **Window Coverings:** None

Chapter 5

Mixing It Up

While choosing colors from a narrow portion of the color wheel has its advantages, as explored in the two preceding chapters, there's also a lot to be said for mixing things up. In this chapter, we'll explore one more way of using the color wheel—zeroing in on complementary schemes, those that pull from opposite sides of the circle. Then we'll look at what happens when you throw the color wheel out the window, ignore the notion that things need to match in order to cohabitate, and let color happen more organically.

Complementary Schemes

Complements are colors that sit directly across the color wheel from each other. So where analogous schemes tend to result in either warm or cool environments, given that they're drawn from only one part of the spectrum, complementary schemes are inherently more balanced. It's like dessert: rather than having to choose between cold ice cream and warm pie, you get to savor what happens when you combine the two.

Opposites and Offsets

Combining opposite colors, though they are natural foils, can be a little tricky, particularly when pairing the primary colors (red, blue, and yellow) with their complements (green, orange, and purple, respectively). Used at full saturation in large doses, the duos can be a bit much. But there are lots of ways to tweak your choices and come up with appealing combinations.

Say you're a fan of green and you don't want to do a monochromatic or analogous scheme, but you're not wild about green with red. Look at ways to throw the combination off a bit. One option is to consider shades other than true red and true green. A lighter green, particularly a dusty shade like sage, looks great with red. And maybe you'd also use a lighter red (a.k.a. pink) or a very dark one. Another strategy is to rotate positions on the wheel in one direction or the other from two key colors. For example, instead of green and red, try blue-green and red-orange or, going the other direction, yellow-green and red-violet. You might also stick with your original shade, true green, and shift just the red, toward either red-orange or red-violet. Or you might use multiple shades of both colors. In other words, pick from the various shades surrounding your key colors rather than limiting yourself to precisely two or getting stuck on their exact relationships on the wheel.

Another alternative is to do a split-complement scheme. Split complements involve three colors rather than just two: your key color plus the two colors that sit on either side of its complement. Sticking with the green example, instead of pairing it with its complement, red, you'd use red's two neighbors, red-orange and red-violet. Or, vice versa, pair red with the two colors on either side of green: yellow-green and blue-green. Of course, as with any scheme, you should feel free to fudge it—play around with variations of the colors until you arrive at a combination that feels right for you.

OPPOSITE PAGE AND THIS PAGE, TOP Complements sometimes work best when used in small doses and/or when using off shades of the colors, like these variations on blue and orange.

BOTTOM LEFT Instead of true purple and true yellow in equal strengths, try a redder purple and a lighter yellow.

BOTTOM RIGHT Yellow-orange and yellow-green are the split complements of purple. Consider it a jumping-off point and tinker with the shades.

TOP LEFT A bold tropical print combines red with blue-green and two shades of yellow-green. The walls repeat the lighter of the yellow-greens.

BOTTOM LEFT Don't be afraid to throw off a complementary pairing—by using orange and green rather than red-orange and blue-green, for example—or to use light and dark shades of your choices.

OPPOSITE PAGE A casual scheme of loosely analogous colors—yellow, gray-green, neon green, and blue-green—gets a jolt from a rug that brings in green's complement, red.

Up to this point, we've focused largely on the notion of a *color scheme,* looking at ways to pick colors that you can then go out and find in the form of paint, fabrics, and so on. But some of the most interesting rooms are those that have no discernible scheme—where the color occurs more organically.

Mixing vs. Matching

In shopping for fabrics or wallpapers, you will inevitably run across matched sets—that is, multiple patterns using the same color palette. It might be fabrics in a stripe, a check, and a floral; or a pair of wallpaper patterns with a matching border. These represent a very simple way to put things together knowing they'll match, because that's what they're designed to do. While it's an impersonal approach (your neighbor might wind up with the exact same thing), it can be a very quick and reliable way to arrive at a color and pattern solution—and for some people, there's nothing more appealing than a perfect match.

However, opinions on whether things should be mixed or matched are as varied as those on whether a home should be soothing or energizing: it's purely subjective. Designer Robin Bell, for instance, is a mixer, never a matcher. "In my office," she says, "nobody is allowed to hold up two swatches next to each other to see if they match. You don't necessarily see things close together like that when you walk into a room." She generally likes an eclectic mix of colors and patterns, but she also prefers a room that looks like it's evolved over time—as if incorporating some antique finds and family heirlooms, none of which would have been upholstered in matching or coordinating fabrics. So her strategy isn't to line swatches up on a board; instead, with a wall color chosen and kept in mind, she pretends her office is the room in question. "If we know the sofa is going to be on the far left, then we throw the sofa fabric over there. If another piece on the opposite side will be upholstered, we'll throw that fabric over there. We look at things as they will appear in the room. Often when you pick up those swatches and look at them together, they actually clash, but the way they relate in the space is perfect." Not only does she not pick a rug—or any other pattern—and then pull colors from it, she likes it when the rug doesn't match. "It's like art. Somebody should be able to give you a rug and you just put it on the floor. Often when a thing appears not to work, it's what pulls the room together." In other words, a little happenstance can make a room special.

OPPOSITE PAGE Red, blue, and green look nice together. There's no rule that the green has to appear in the rug to make sense on the wall.

TOP RIGHT This room is mixed *and* matched. The walls match the blue paisley print, while the rug is a different pattern and palette, with only a hint of blue.

BOTTOM RIGHT While green and blue are clearly the dominant hues, the cushion, pillow, throw, and paintings all harmonize rather than match.

ABOVE The chairs, throw pillow, and window frame simply pick up on the most prominent of the quilt's striking colors.

LEFT The scene on a classic Chinese lantern sets the palette for the living room.

OPPOSITE PAGE Green plaid, mauve velvet, salmon satin—this inventive combination follows cues from the decorative panel on the celadon-colored wall, without exactly matching it.

Readymade Palettes

Perhaps the best way to arrive at unpredictable—even unorthodox—color combinations that work is to let someone else do the picking for you. Maybe it is a matter of pulling colors out of a rug pattern. Or maybe it's about noticing a bowl of marbles, or a mural on a restaurant wall, or a jumble of flowers—something that speaks to you—and building your color scheme from that. Some of the best combinations are those you might never have thought of. Appropriate them from wherever you find them, and then make them your own by varying the shades or mixing in patterns that don't quite match. Or, in the case of a textile or painting with its own distinctive colors, you might opt to simply leave it at that, only choosing a wall color or a few accent pieces that enhance its already brilliant scheme.

Playing Complements

THIS PAGE AND OPPOSITE PAGE, RIGHT Saturated blue and orange can be garish together. Here they're used in the perfect amounts.

OPPOSITE PAGE, LEFT The sleeping loft's quaint antique beds make sense in the house because of their color.

There's a constant thread of blue running through this Southern California home (see also the master bedroom on pages 112–113), but its prevalence and partnerships vary from room to room. In the living room, blue is paired with its complement, a nice bold orange. Here, the blue acts as the secondary shade, coming in the singular form of a peacock-blue lamp base. But take the ladder up to the sleeping loft and not only does blue become the dominant color—this time in a lighter shade—but the orange shifts to pink. The charming, tole-painted antique beds might seem like a stylistic departure, but the blue gives them a reason to be here. Striped pillows and the glimpse of brighter, more modern blue linens help tie the beds in with the rest of the house.

The Elements

■ **Walls:** White-painted paneling

■ **Ceiling:** White-painted boards

■ **Floors:** Hardwood, with faded brown-and-blue rug

■ **Furnishings:** White-upholstered sofas and armchair; zebra-upholstered bench and footstool; dark-wood coffee table and end tables; faded-blue antique twin beds

■ **Window Coverings:** None

■ **Accents:** Downstairs, orange throw and pillows plus blue ceramic lamp; upstairs, cerulean-blue bedding with white blankets and blue-and-pink striped pillows

Key-Lime Kitchen

THIS PAGE The dark-wood floor and counters offset the cool tones of lime, aqua, and steel.

OPPOSITE PAGE, LEFT The hutch combines the lime and aqua, while its hot-pink interior spices things up.

OPPOSITE PAGE, RIGHT Classic Florida colors and patterns—and a bit of gingerbread trim—contribute to the sense that the kitchen is older than it is.

In this newly built Florida Keys kitchen, designed to look as if it has been here for decades, the walls were painted the color of key lime pie, and the traditional frame-and-panel cabinetry a soothing aqua. Light and dark notes come, respectively, from the white of the ceiling and trim, and the dark-stained Dade County pine of the floor and countertops. But the real tropical punch comes from reaching across the color wheel from the blue and yellow-green, and adding a jolt of hot pink. While dishware in a mix of yellows, greens, and blues is displayed on open shelves, the pink appears only in the interior and trim of the recessed storage hutch (which has drawers and doorframes painted the same shade as the walls). Containing that treatment to the hutch allows it to be a spot of eccentricity in the otherwise cool, calm room.

The Elements

- **Walls:** Pale yellow-green

- **Ceiling:** White-painted planks

- **Floors:** Dark-stained pine

- **Countertops:** Salvaged pine

- **Cabinets:** Painted aqua; hutch with hot-pink interior and trim, yellow-green door trim and drawer fronts

- **Appliances:** Stainless steel

- **Window Coverings:** None

- **Accents:** Dishware in shades of yellow, green, and blue; multihued table linens; vintage milk-glass light fixture; steel drainboard sink

The Art of the Clash

THIS PAGE The major elements of the room—walls, shelves, sofa, chairs—are almost utilitarian, a perfect backdrop for the rugs, fabrics, and artifacts.

OPPOSITE PAGE, TOP AND BOTTOM The gray concrete of the fireplace and kitchen "cabinets" remains neutral while holding its own. The exotic doors on the kitchen echo the rugs used throughout the house.

This spare white-and-concrete home is laden with treasures from around the globe, all underscored by an eclectic but cohesive collection of textiles—rugs, pillows, and a suzani thrown over the back of the basic white couch. What makes the mix work is that, no matter the origin or ethnicity of the various textiles, all are multihued but with some shade of red as the dominant color. It also makes a certain inherent visual sense, because in the parts of the world these items are collected from or inspired by, there is not the emphasis on "matching" that one finds in the United States. Rather, the impulse is simply to relish color and pattern and throw them together with abandon, allowing them to clash or harmonize as they will.

At the entrance to the kitchen, a pair of ornate, carved doors continues the theme. Again multihued and with a preponderance of red, the doors feel almost like another pair of carpets, stood on end.

The Elements

- **Walls and Ceiling:** White

- **Floors:** Dark-stained and polished concrete

- **Countertops and Open Shelves:** Concrete

- **Furnishings:** White sofa; reddish-brown leather club chairs; ornate imported wood accent tables and prayer chair

- **Window Coverings:** Wood shutters

- **Accents:** Rugs, pillows, and blankets in a mix of ethnic patterns, all predominantly red; ornate carved and multicolored doors; artifacts of all kinds and from all over

THIS PAGE The room's color scheme is one of split complements—blue and green paired with orange.

OPPOSITE PAGE A mix of cabinet surfaces creates interest in the modestly sized kitchen, while white upper cabinets almost disappear, making the space feel bigger than it is.

For his San Francisco client with an interest in architecture and design, John Lum built a combination living room–kitchen in shades of black, white, and wood. The architecture provides a handsome showcase for the homeowner's collections of midcentury furnishings, paintings, and photographs; objects from around the world; and a colorful collection of enameled bowls, which are displayed on open shelves. It's a room that wears its color scheme lightly, but there are repeating elements of blue and green and their opposite, red-orange. The threads of blue and orange, in particular, along with the grays of the cabinetry and the off-white paneling, help link the room to the older parts of the home, seen on pages 174–175.

The Elements

- **Walls:** Off-white V-groove paneling

- **Ceiling:** Wood in the living room; white in the kitchen

- **Floors:** Blond hardwood

- **Countertops:** Off-white engineered stone

- **Cabinets:** Glossy white uppers; matte dark-gray base cabinets and island (with steel grates mounted on three sides); matte medium-gray pantry wall; open cookbook niche with shelves painted orange on the bottom and blue on the top

- **Appliances:** Stainless-steel range, hood, and countertop appliances; refrigerator faced to match surrounding gray cabinets

- **Furnishings:** Gray-and-tan–tweed sofa; charcoal-gray high-backed chair; burnt-orange armchair; white-and-marble Saarinen coffee table; carved-wood side table

- **Window Coverings:** None

- **Accents:** Blackened-steel fireplace; white globe light; blue-gray rug; large blue-and-green painting; enameled bowl collection; assorted throw pillows

A Spot of Whimsy

THIS PAGE The brightly patterned floral of the barstools plays beautifully off the nearly neutral mosaic-tile wall.

OPPOSITE PAGE The pink daybed cushion is a nod to the original kitchen counters, while the white-metal furniture hints at the adjacent garden.

When Charles De Lisle embarked on the renovation of this vacation home, he knew it needed to be fun. "The kitchen originally had pink laminate countertops—very '50s—and the client wanted to retain some of that kooky playfulness. It was important to her that we inject that color back into the house. Not in a kitschy '50s way, but not in a completely contemporary way either." His solution takes the form of a lively mosaic wall at one end of the room and a white wrought-iron daybed at the other, outfitted with a pink cushion and multicolored pillows.

The tile wall is gray, brown, white, ivory, and yellow; and pulled up to the island counter are barstools with seats in the same vivacious pink, orange, blue, and yellow print that's on the daybed's throw pillows. The tile and fabric have just two things in common: a spot of yellow and a funky attitude. That creates more intrigue than if they matched. Of course, there are ample neutral underpinnings, which keep it all on the sophisticated side of kooky.

The Elements

- **Walls:** White-painted adobe; ceiling-high tile backsplash in neutrals plus yellow
- **Ceiling:** Wood beams and rafters
- **Floors:** Concrete, with natural-fiber rug
- **Countertops:** Terrazzo
- **Cabinets:** Wood frames with off-white doors; island front painted dark gray
- **Appliances:** Stainless steel
- **Furnishings:** Asymmetrical wood table; white-coated metal chairs with caramel leather pads; bamboo barstools with floral seats; white-coated iron daybed with pink cushion; natural wood-block accent tables
- **Window Coverings:** None
- **Accents:** Multicolored throw pillows; custom light fixtures

Studied Elegance

THIS PAGE Red, orange, and brown create a warm environment, tempered a bit by cool blue-grays.

OPPOSITE PAGE Among the many patterns, the feminine toile is countered by the masculine glen plaid. The X-pattern of brass nailheads adds another handsome touch.

BIRDS OF THE WORLD

Setting out to create an ultra-cozy spot to curl up with a good book, the designer of this small study layered on the colors, textures, and patterns, variously mixing and matching the parts. She warmed up the space—a spare bedroom that doubles as a guest room—with dark-brown grass-cloth walls, then applied even darker brown paint to the ceilings, window trim, and baseboards. The dark floor is covered with a natural-fiber rug. Into this brown haven, she placed an orange leather chair, cinnabar-colored nesting tables, and a daybed upholstered in tan and glen plaid. A toile pattern is confined to the corniced canopy behind the daybed, and the daybed is topped with pillows in solids, patterns, and more glen plaid—all in shades of brown, blue-gray, and orange. It's an elegant example of the artfully controlled mix.

The Elements

- **Walls:** Dark-brown grass cloth

- **Ceiling and Trim:** Painted brown

- **Floors:** Hardwood with natural-fiber rug

- **Furnishings:** Orange leather club chair; brass side table; red nesting tables; daybed upholstered in tan and glen plaid, with brass nailheads

- **Window Coverings:** Tortoiseshell blinds

- **Accents:** Taxidermy; vintage brown-plaid suitcases; chrome swing-arm reading lamp; throw pillows in a variety of colors and patterns

Laissez-Faire Look

Case Study

THIS PAGE Two florals and a stripe mix amicably, while the blue bench fabric repeats as a pillow.

OPPOSITE PAGE, TOP A green armoire and gray-and-white–striped chair continue themes from the living room but are set against a dramatic wall color.

OPPOSITE PAGE, BOTTOM The black floor sets off the light-colored furnishings.

In Tia Zoldan's view, a neutral backdrop makes it easy to experiment with lots of color and pattern, and the impact of this philosophy is evident in her own home. Starting with a base of white walls, black-stained floors, simple seagrass rugs, and a matched white sofa, armchair, and ottoman, she mixes accent furnishings and decorative elements unreservedly. Of course, there is a little bit of method to her madness: there are neutral browns; there are black-and-white patterns; and there are shades of blue and green. With a few minor ground rules established, though, she simply has fun with it.

The Elements

- **Walls:** White in the living room; tobacco in the dining room

- **Ceilings:** White

- **Floors:** Hardwood stained black, with seagrass rugs

- **Furnishings:** Matching white upholstered sofa, armchair, and ottoman; blue button-tufted bench with oversized nailheads; Barcelona chair and cube footstool covered in beige tweed; ottoman upholstered in black-and-white floral pattern with black welt; brass campaign table; assorted wood and metal accent tables; wicker trunk; black dining table; white-linen slipcovered dining chairs; white side chairs upholstered in wide gray stripe with brass nailheads

- **Window Coverings:** White curtains in the living room; none in the dining room

- **Accents:** Assorted artworks; throw pillows in various patterns and colors; zebra-hide rug; glazed white garden stool; nickel table lamp; aged-brass chandelier

Chapter 6

Going Bold

Most designers concur that color is the quickest way to animate a room. And if you're talking about paint, it can also be the cheapest way; it's certainly less expensive than new upholstery or flooring. But using bold colors and/or using color boldly—not necessarily the same thing—takes a bold personality. If white walls and soft colors are not for you, you've come to the right chapter. The unabashedly colorful rooms in the following pages are broken down into graphic rooms, dramatic rooms, and exotic rooms.

Graphic Color

Black walls with white windows and shelving make a graphic backdrop for a striped slipper chair and lemon-yellow stool.

Graphic color is a term describing flat fields of color used geometrically (say, in stripes or grid-based patterns) or to emphasize the form or geometry of an object (such as an egg-shaped yellow chair or a blue orb of a lamp). Most often, the colors used in a graphic scheme are quite saturated, but that's certainly not always the case, as seen here. What does hold true is that the use of graphic techniques imparts instant dynamism to a space, by virtue of its bold embrace of form and color.

ABOVE LEFT A bright geometric panel, marked off in a grid, stands in for a headboard.

TOP RIGHT Juicy colors emphasize the geometric forms of the sideboard, lamp, and chair.

BOTTOM RIGHT Variously colored fronts turn six vanity drawers into a playful design.

TOP LEFT Yellow curtains and an orange couch are made even bolder by a pair of geometrically patterned pillows.

TOP RIGHT A single bold, red form—here the rectangular kitchen island—is enough to energize any space.

BOTTOM Bold stripes—inspired by a grosgrain ribbon—change the dynamic of this girls' room.

OPPOSITE PAGE Flat fields of color on the near cabinets and far wall pull your gaze through the space.

Dramatic Color

There are those of us who like our rooms to remain in the background and those who prefer that they have big personalities of their own. This might mean using lots of bold colors in daring combinations, or it might mean using deep, sophisticated colors in quite lavish ways. But color is undoubtedly the shortest route to a dramatic setting.

"Color is probably the most emotional thing that people respond to" in the realm of interior design, says Michael Bell. "An English-arm sofa versus a rolled-arm sofa, not an emotional response. *Red* is an emotional response. You show somebody red, orange, yellow, they're going to react to it. So color is how you can create a response and get the most bang for your buck." That said, everyone has ideas about which rooms are best suited to dramatic color treatments. As Bell says, "I think there are rooms that simply lend themselves to being more

dramatic." High on our experts' list of such spaces are dining rooms and powder rooms. Tia Zoldan thinks people tend to want some drama in their dining rooms because they're often only used when entertaining. "And in the powder room," says Charles De Lisle, "I usually do something crazy. Because that's the little room that, when you have guests over, they get to go witness the craziness."

It's a challenge to create drama in a room with white walls, but take even the most neutral mix of furnishings and set them against boldly colored walls, and now you've got drama. If you're working with paint and keeping it to walls (as opposed to large banks of kitchen cabinets, for instance), it won't represent a big investment either to do it or to change it later, so there's really no reason not to experiment. If you're working with something more permanent—stone or tile—be sure you'll like the color long enough for the investment to make sense.

OPPOSITE PAGE
Dusky midnight-blue walls set a glamorous tone in Lisa Rowe's formal living room.

ABOVE LEFT If you're going to be as bold as the green tile in this Deco-style bathroom, be sure your love for the color will last.

TOP RIGHT
Chocolate-brown walls and an ornate mirror turn Lisa Rowe's standard-issue powder room into a gem.

BOTTOM RIGHT
Deep-purple paint on all four walls plays up the architectural drama of this room.

TOP Chairs painted the same brilliant blue as the walls and ceiling add extra punch to this dining room.

BOTTOM LEFT A blue-black exterior wall makes a dramatic backdrop for an outdoor living room.

BOTTOM RIGHT Terra-cotta walls and expansive blue-and-white tile make for a unique kitchen.

RIGHT White furnishings and bright-yellow accents pop out from Lee Kleinhelter's cozy cave of a bedroom.

Exotic Color

LEFT Simply borrowing an exotic color combination—like the faded black, worn blue-greens, and vibrant orange here—can transform a room.

RIGHT Even if you don't copy Mexico's favorite shades, you might be influenced by the piling on of patterns in Mexican interiors.

Whether English chintz or Asian lacquer, color is used in different ways by different cultures. The color sensibility of a place is often heavily influenced by its landscape and plant life. Tuscany is heavily associated with terra-cotta–tile roofs and olive orchards, for instance, whereas in Hawaii it's the blue of the ocean and the bright hues of tropical blooms. "I am a big advocate of travel and exposure," says Michael Bell, when asked how one might hone one's color sense. "If you go to Italy, you are affected by the colors. If you go to Bali, there is color everywhere—pink and orange."

Observing the colors of other countries and cultures can broaden your sense of the possibilities or even suggest combinations you can use to evoke your favorite places when you're back at home. The tropical pattern on your hotel-room sofa may not make sense back in the Berkshires, but pink, blue, and orange pillows on your tan couch might ignite some of the pleasure the vacation gave you—or make you feel like you've been somewhere you may never get to. If there's a land you love, study it—look at the colors in photos and in other interiors that draw on that place, and find ways to use them in your own rooms.

TOP LEFT The Eastern influence can be as simple as lots of wood and red lacquer.

TOP RIGHT Western-style sofas dressed in Asian prints combine with Chinese Chippendale chairs and red stools for an East-meets-West effect.

BOTTOM LEFT Exuberantly colored fabrics and a paper parasol recreate Bali in a backyard.

BOTTOM RIGHT A mix of vibrant Indian fabrics makes an exotic locale out of this Southern California porch.

OPPOSITE PAGE This jewel-toned room reflects a Middle Eastern influence.

THIS PAGE The bright-green island makes an instant focal point of the kitchen.

OPPOSITE PAGE, TOP There's a certain symmetry about a third-story wall of windows opposite one painted sky blue.

OPPOSITE PAGE, BOTTOM Lime-green chairs draw the eye out to the deck, tying the indoor and outdoor spaces together.

"Contemporary architecture doesn't mean you have to live in museum- or art gallery–like settings," says John Lum. "The goal with this house was to create a warm, hospitable environment." What better way to do that than by combining large expanses of wood with friendly colors like lime green and sky blue? That's exactly what Lum and his team did.

In the open living-dining-kitchen area, the floors and counters are concrete; shelves and partitions are blackened steel; and contrasting wood-tones make up the ceilings and cabinetry—medium-toned hardwood on the former and, on the latter, a dark-wood photo-laminate sandwiched behind glass. With the space on the top floor of the three-story structure, the dining area features a wall of windows to take in the city view. Opposite the window wall is a solid wall painted blue, while the prominently placed island is bright green. With so much architectural color, the bulk of the furnishings were kept neutral, punctuated by colored chairs in strategic spots. Altogether, it's a rich tapestry of colors and surfaces. Lum sums it up nicely: "We're definitely not minimalists."

The Elements

- **Walls:** White, sky blue, and wood-grain laminate behind glass

- **Ceiling:** FSC-certified tropical hardwood

- **Floors:** Concrete with hardwood "hallway"

- **Countertops:** Concrete

- **Cabinets:** Glass-fronted wood veneer; lime-green island

- **Furnishings:** Armless sofas and side chairs with neutral upholstery; bamboo barstools; dining chairs in white and blue; lime-green molded-plastic deck chairs

- **Window Coverings:** None

- **Accents:** Built-in steel shelf/planter as room divider; mirrored globe light fixtures

Of the Earth

THIS PAGE Red optically lowers a ceiling, so it works in a room like this one with a very high ceiling.

OPPOSITE PAGE, TOP LEFT A red-velvet Victorian chair heightens the drama.

OPPOSITE PAGE, TOP RIGHT White trim would spoil the mood in the dining room; the green is much softer. A subtle shift in color emphasizes the coved ceiling.

The owners of this Portland, Oregon, home love color so much they founded a nontoxic-paint company, and their wholehearted embrace of color is evident in every room. Having chosen a loose palette of earthy greens, ochers, reds, and red-oranges—earthy colors being their specialty—they use them liberally but in varying ways from one room to the next, with Venetian plaster lending the colors added dimension along the way. The kitchen, for instance, is a pale gold with leaf-green cabinets, ocher trim, and a red ceiling, while the moodier dining room is drenched in terra-cotta, with a two-tone ceiling set off by trim the same green as the kitchen cabinets. The result is rooms that, rather than matching, hang together in a casual, almost offhand way.

The Elements

- **Walls:** Venetian plaster in varying shades

- **Ceilings:** Matte paint in varying shades

- **Floors:** Hardwood; parquet in dining room

- **Countertops:** Butcher block

- **Cabinets:** Painted leaf green

- **Furnishings:** Classic Cherner chairs at wood-topped dining table with wrought-iron base; Victorian side chair; wood chest of drawers

- **Window Coverings:** None

- **Accents:** Vintage butcher block as island; Victorian table lamp; rustic metal chandeliers

A Meeting of Minds

THIS PAGE The
blue wall is equal
parts soothing and
energizing.

OPPOSITE PAGE
De Lisle added pink
cushions to the
vintage sofa, and
his client found the
brown floral rug.

"She really likes vibrant color," says Charles De Lisle, referring to the owner of this home office, and that's evident at first glance. When the two set out to redo the room—a long, ground-floor space, with windows at only one end—they knew they wanted it to be bright and lively, and both designer and client are fans of bold and unpredictable color combinations. For the wall her desk sits against, the client chose a blue that's light but not wan—like robin's-egg with an attitude. For the opposite wall, De Lisle suggested a vivid, grapefruit-yellow color called parakeet, which he then "messed up" with a hand-brushed coating of satin polyurethane. "Otherwise, that color looks really plastic," he says, "so we wanted to tone it down a bit." The result is a stimulating work space and a showcase for the client's other occupation: an extensive, years-in-the-making collection of sailors, portraits, mermaids, and vintage movie posters.

The Elements

- **Walls:** Bright robin's-egg blue on one wall; bright grapefruit on opposite wall, with satin polyurethane coating that was hand-brushed every which way while still wet

- **Floors:** Blond hardwood

- **Furnishings:** Maple desk and open shelf; iconic aluminum Navy chairs; vintage sofa covered in nubby reddish-pink fabric, with added pink cushions; steel side table

- **Accents:** Pinboard covered in greenish-khaki cloth; collections of sailors, portraits, mermaids, and movie posters (the latter two not shown), along with personal photos, postcards, and other mementos

**THIS PAGE AND OPPOSITE, BOTTOM
LEFT** Orange accents play off the shade-
shifting gray in the bedroom.

**OPPOSITE PAGE, TOP AND BOTTOM
RIGHT** In the dining room and bathroom,
the blue ceiling actually begins at the
picture rail. Ivory wainscoting reduces the
volume of the stronger wall colors.

The handful of rooms in this handsome Edwardian flat all draw from the same palette of paints—an ivory, a warm gray, a pale blue, a dark khaki, and a bright orange—but each room features them in a different combination, imparting complexity to them along the way. The bedroom is gray with a khaki ceiling, and is accessed by ivory pocket doors. The dining room, on the other hand, is orange with ivory wainscoting and a blue ceiling, while the bathroom is gray, but with the same ivory wainscoting and blue ceiling. The blue and orange react differently to each other than the blue and gray, for example, and all of the colors change according to the light in each room. The gray is warmer in the bathroom than in the bedroom, where the color shifts dramatically just from the top of the wall to the bottom. It's a study in how seductive dramatic colors can be in low-light space. (See also the bay window on page 70.)

The Elements

- **Walls:** Variously orange, gray, and ivory

- **Ceilings:** Blue and khaki; ivory ceiling medallion in dining room

- **Floors:** Hardwood; wall-to-wall sisal in dining room; gray tile in bathroom

- **Furnishings:** Platform bed with woven rush headboard; orange lacquer bedside table; vintage wooden dining table, sideboard, and chairs with black leather seats and backs

- **Window Coverings:** Ivory blinds

- **Accents:** Brown-and-white shams and duvet cover; orange blanket; yellow-orange bolsters; chrome task lamp; bronze globe pendant fixture; midcentury silver tea service; oversized imported metal candlesticks; assorted artwork

Tropical Delight

THIS PAGE It would be hard to wake up on the wrong side of the bed in a room this rosy.

OPPOSITE PAGE, TOP A softer version of the bedroom's palette sets a calmer tone in the bath.

OPPOSITE PAGE, BOTTOM The hallmark of a Florida interior is the wall-mounted fish.

When a *Smithsonian* magazine editor and his wife decided to renovate a Key West, Florida, cottage to retire to from Washington DC, they gave the local palette the full embrace, combining lots of light blues and jungle greens with expanses of local pine. Not shy about using pink—and in a place like Key West, there's no need to be—they painted both the exterior of the home and their master bath a pale pink, and painted their bedroom a more vivid shade of the color. Blue, green, striped, and tropical-print bedding are echoed in a series of doors, each a different color. Cuban-style concrete tiles in the bathroom pick up the same palette in slightly softer shades. White trim and accents keep things bright and help tie the spaces together.

The Elements

- **Walls:** Bright pink in the bedroom; soft pink in the bathroom

- **Ceiling:** Medium-stained wood planks

- **Floors:** Reclaimed heart pine with natural-fiber rug; patterned concrete tile

- **Furnishings:** Upholstered headboard in light apple-green; white wicker side table

- **Accents:** White ceiling fan and bed linens; green-and-white quilt; pillows in stripes, solids, and florals; nickel-plated reading lights; black-and-white Hemingway photos; wall-mounted mahimahi

East Meets West Coast

THIS PAGE Bamboo-faced drawers, a jewel-toned bed, a pink-peony painting, and a parasol evoke Southeast Asia.

OPPOSITE PAGE, TOP Light-colored bamboo poles stand out against the dark ceiling and cabinetry.

OPPOSITE PAGE, BOTTOM LEFT Above the deep-green sofa with ruby pillows hangs a painting found in a Philippines street market.

OPPOSITE PAGE, BOTTOM RIGHT The Asian aesthetic is applied indoors and out.

The owner of this houseboat spent years living and traveling in Southeast Asia before settling down in the waters of Hayden Island, Oregon. Her home is filled with mementos brought back from Asia, but even more, it's imbued with an Asian-tropical color palette and aesthetic. Part global street market, part Zen temple, it is designed around lots of wood and bamboo, joined by rich jewel tones in the upholstery and bedding. The ceilings are covered in reed screens from the hardware store, the beams stained a deep reddish-brown. Along with wood walls and Cambodian floor mats, these touches turn the tiny boat into something undeniably exotic.

The same color sense and aesthetic carry over to the deck, which is about half the size of the house and extends the space for living and entertaining. Surrounded by lush plants from both East and West, a sunken dining area houses benches with plush green cushions and ruby throw pillows.

The Elements

- **Walls:** Dark-wood planks, running on the horizontal in some spaces and on the vertical in others

- **Ceiling:** Shellacked reed screens and stained beams

- **Floors:** Light-toned hardwood with Cambodian mats

- **Countertops:** Black tile and blond wood

- **Cabinets:** Stained dark red-brown

- **Appliances:** Stainless steel

- **Furnishings:** Emerald-green sofa; built-in bed with zebra-patterned headboard and ruby- and sapphire-colored bedding and curtains

- **Window Coverings:** Sheer, off-white café curtains

- **Accents:** Asian plates on stands; dishware in shades of yellow and green; wicker, rattan, and iron barstools; paper parasol as light fixture; scenic and floral paintings found in Asian street markets; lamps with Buddha-head and fish bases

Black, White, and Blue

THIS PAGE The blue wall sets off the bold form of the substantial, black four-poster bed.

OPPOSITE PAGE, LEFT White vinyl takes the stuffiness out of a wingback chair.

OPPOSITE PAGE, RIGHT Ceramics and patterned drapes brighten the guest bedroom.

When a designer with a popular television show bought a loft by the beach in Santa Monica, he wanted to retain its sense of spaciousness but not the industrial vibe. Having been told he was scared of bright colors, he decided to fill the space with black and white furnishings set against vivid walls and mixed with brightly colored objects. He had two bedrooms walled off and painted the shade of blue that researchers must surely be talking about when they say people feel happier in rooms with blue walls. Old-fashioned molding applied to the walls in the master bedroom is treated to the same color. Baseboards in both rooms are painted white, creating a crisp border between walls and floors. The mix of strong black and white pieces pops against this serene background, while vibrantly hued pillows, lamps, and vases make it lively.

The Elements

- **Walls:** Painted blue, with white baseboards

- **Floors:** Warm-brown hardwood

- **Furnishings:** Black four-poster bed; black chest of drawers with white top; metal stools with black patent button-tufted seats; white vinyl wingback chair with brass nailheads; glossy-white side table; white-lacquer Asian chest of drawers on black base; white ornamental side chair

- **Window Coverings:** Black-and-white–patterned floor-length drapes

- **Accents:** White bedding with black border; throw pillows in bright salmon, zebra, and a blue-green-yellow op-art pattern; cowhide rug; blue-ceramic lamp base; yellow-glazed vases

Let the Sunshine In

THIS PAGE The yellow walls convey the same happy-go-luckiness as the jumble of patterns and colors.

OPPOSITE PAGE The leather butterfly chair and sisal carpet keep everything else in check.

It takes confidence with color to take a bunch of things that have no right to be in the same room, throw them all together, and come up with something magic. This New York City apartment gets its sunny disposition from walls the color of dandelions. Sisal carpeting adds to the cheerful and relaxed demeanor. And then comes a riot of colors and patterns that looks anything but riotous: a red throw over the couch, topped with patterned pillows in pink and yellow, purple and yellow, green and pink; a table draped in an exotic-print tablecloth of green, blue, and red; a butterfly chair in brown leather; and an armchair in a wacky playing-cards–and–poker-chips pattern, finished with bright red piping. It's just crazy enough to work.

The Elements

- **Walls:** Dandelion yellow with white trim

- **Floors:** Wall-to-wall sisal

- **Furnishings:** Sofa with red throw; brown-leather butterfly chair; casino-print armchair; baby grand piano with Far East chair

- **Window Coverings:** None

- **Accents:** Weathered white Asian coffee table; Chinese pottery in blue-and-white and green-and-rose patterns; mismatched throw pillows; patterned tablecloth; antique side table; ivory lamp with black shade

Sugar and Spice

THIS PAGE Faced with pink and orange stripes, a wall of storage becomes a decorative element.

OPPOSITE PAGE, LEFT A pink-and-brown floral print and a bright-blue floor make an idiosyncratic combo.

OPPOSITE PAGE, RIGHT The work space sets a playful mood, with bright-yellow walls and mix-and-match cabinet fronts.

ownstairs from the living space on pages 168–169, John Lum created a girl's bedroom and adjoining craft room like no other. Rather than making it overly girly—and thus likely to need a complete makeover in a couple of years—he created a bold, graphic background that will withstand a change of furnishings, art, and bed linens as the little girl enters her teenage years. For now, sweet pink-and-brown linens on a streamlined steel twin bed strike a balance between cute and modern.

It's hard to say which is most striking: the puzzle-piece floor tiles in turquoise concrete; the pink-and-orange striped storage wall; or the desk unit in the craft room, with its face panels of orange and blue laminate.

The Elements

- **Walls:** White in the bedroom; bright yellow in the craft room

- **Floors:** Blue concrete tile with contrasting gray grout

- **Cabinets:** Faced with multicolored laminate

- **Furnishings:** Steel bed; chrome and wood desk; chrome and white-laminate side table; yellow task chair

- **Accents:** Magenta stool; orange metal trash can and storage bin; pink, brown, and white floral bedding; deer pillow

Color Wheel and Glossary

As discussed on page 17, the color wheel is a visual representation of the colors of the spectrum, and it illustrates the color terms and concepts defined below. The second ring of the wheel holds the key colors—primary, secondary, and tertiary—with darker shades on the outside and progressively lighter ones moving toward the center. Each ring contains colors of the same value.

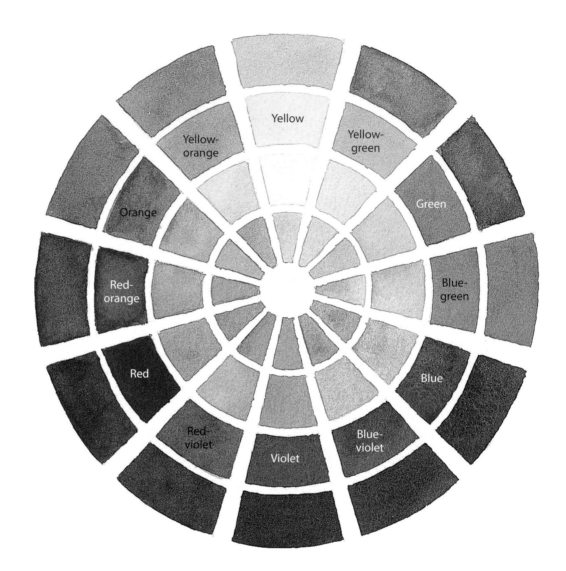

ANALOGOUS COLORS
Colors that sit next to each other on the color wheel

COMPLEMENTARY COLORS
Colors that sit directly across from each other on the color wheel, such as blue and orange

COOL COLOR A color from the half of the spectrum or color wheel ranging from yellow-green through purple

HUE A synonym for *color*

PALETTE Any set of colors chosen as the basis around which to design a room

PRIMARY COLOR Any of the three colors from which all other colors are derived—namely red, blue, and yellow

SATURATION The relative level of a color's pigmentation (e.g., kelly green is more saturated than mint green)

SECONDARY COLOR A color achieved by blending any two primary colors—namely purple (a.k.a. violet, the result of mixing red and blue), green (blue and yellow), and orange (yellow and red)

SHADE A variation on any key color arrived at by lightening it with white and/ or darkening it with black

SPECTRUM The range of visible colors, as seen in the rainbow or when light is bent through a prism

SPLIT COMPLEMENTS The two colors that sit on either side of any color's complement (e.g., purple's split complements are yellow-orange and yellow-green, its complement being yellow)

TERTIARY COLOR A color achieved by blending a primary color with one of its secondary derivatives (e.g., red and orange combine to make red-orange)

VALUE The relative lightness or darkness of a color; see also *Saturation*

WARM COLOR A color from the half of the spectrum or color wheel ranging from red-purple through yellow

ROBERTS | ECHO   Time at Home

John Welsh **Modern House**

the minimalist garden christopher bradley-hole

THE **family home**   Copestick

vitra.

Credits

Photography

Edmund Barr: 30 top; **Gordon Beall:** 5 bottom left; **Adam Belanger:** 5 top right; **Fernando Bengoechea/Beateworks/Corbis:** 16, 39 bottom right, 43 top left, 48 bottom left, 63 top, 73, 99 bottom right, 101 top left, 138 top; **Carter Berg:** 4 top right; **Rob D. Brodman:** 45 bottom left; **Robbie Caponetto:** 83 top, 150, 151 top, 158 bottom; **August Cenname:** 5 top left; **davidduncanlivingston.com:** 8, 10, 28, 106 top right; **Christopher Drake/Red/Cover:** 67 left; **John Ellis:** 80 top, 90, 91 both; **Pieter Estersohn/Beateworks/Corbis:** 10 bottom left, 14 bottom, 19 bottom left, 19 bottom right, 30 bottom, 33 top, 50, 56 bottom left, 65, 67 top right, 71 top right, 74, 79 bottom, 104, 167, 182, 183 top; **Macduff Everton/Corbis:** 27 center; **Michael Freeman/Red/Cover:** 83 center right; **William Geddes/Beateworks/Corbis:** 57; **David George/Red/Cover:** 68 bottom left, 161 bottom right;

Tria Giovan: 10 top left, 22, 24 left, 37 top, 37 bottom, 42, 43 top right, 48 top, 48 bottom right, 51, 52 top right, 55 bottom, 56 top, 64 bottom right, 71 top left, 72 top left, 72 top right, 78, 81 top, 83 bottom right, 84 top, 85 bottom left, 88, 89 both, 101 top right, 102 bottom right, 105 top, 114, 115 right, 134 top, 142, 143 both, 144, 145 both, 156, 157 top right, 176, 177 both; **John Granen:** 3 middle, 15, 131, 135; **Art Gray:** 45 bottom right, 85 top right, 98, 100 top left, 106 bottom right, 108, 111 bottom right, 122, 123 all, 126, 127 top right, 148, 149 both, 157 bottom right; **Margot Hartford:** 23, 106 bottom left, 139; **Ken Hayden/Red/Cover:** 67 bottom right; **Sandy Lankford:** 5 middle right; **Nicholas Lemonnier/Red Cover:** 1; **Leigh Jae Manacher:** 4 bottom right; **Maura McEvoy:** 2 right, 77, 92, 93 all; **Christine McNeill:** 5 bottom right; **Anastassios Mentas/Red/Cover:** 85 bottom right; **Karyn Millet/Red/Cover:** 72 bottom left, 72 bottom

right; **N. Minh & J. Wass/Red/Cover:** 18, 60 top left, 61, 71 bottom, 134 bottom, 157 left, 158 top left, 161 left; **Lisa Romerein:** 19 top, 25 right, 26, 27 bottom, 37 center, 40 bottom right, 94, 95 both, 100 bottom right, 101 bottom right, 107, 109 top, 112, 113 both, 136, 140, 141 both, 166 bottom right; **Jeremy Samuelson:** 2 left, 3 right, 14 top, 25 left, 29 right, 35, 46, 52 top left, 53, 54, 64 top, 81 bottom right, 102 bottom left, 103, 137 bottom, 152, 153 both, 155, 162 top, 164, 166 top left, 166 bottom left; **Kim Sayer/Red/Cover:** 47 bottom right; **Michael Skott:** 17, 39 bottom left, 44, 80 bottom, 81 bottom left, 99 left, 101 bottom left, 102 top left, 188, 191; **Thomas J. Story:** 7, 10 top right, 12, 13 right, 24, 38, 40 top left, 41, 49, 52 bottom left, 58, 62, 75 top left, 75 top right, 82, 83 bottom left, 106 top left, 111 top right, 111 bottom left, 118, 119 both, 120, 121 all, 128, 129 both, 132, 133 top, 159, 162, 168, 169 both, 170, 171 both, 178, 179

all, 184, 185 both, 187, 192; **Tim Street-Porter:** 14 center, 27 top, 32, 33 bottom, 39 top left, 40 top right, 40 bottom left, 45 top right, 47 left, 55 top, 59, 60 top right, 60 bottom, 63 bottom left, 66, 68 top, 69, 75 bottom, 86, 87 top, 105 bottom right, 110, 124, 125 both, 162 bottom right, 163, 165; **Tim Street-Porter/Beateworks/Corbis:** 36, 52 bottom right, 79 top, 84 bottom, 99 right, 138 bottom, 158 top right; **Dominique Vorillon:** 31 bottom left, 31 bottom right, 43 bottom, 47 top right, 64 bottom left, 105 bottom left, 109 bottom, 137 top, 160, 161 top right, 166 top right, 180, 181 both, 189; **Deborah Whitlaw:** 39 top right; **Michele Lee Willson:** 3 left, 20 both, 21 both, 70, 97, 111 top left, 116, 117 both, 133 bottom left, 133 bottom right, 146, 147 all, 172, 173, 174, 175 all; **Henry Wilson/Red/Cover:** 63 bottom right; **Karen Witynski:** 31 top

Design

1: Vera Cristo; 2 top right: Carl Palasota, carlpalasota@cox.net; 3 top middle: John Schneider and Kim Clements, J.A.S. Design-Build, Seattle, www.jasdesignbuild.com; 7: Yolo Colorhouse, www.yolocolorhouse.com; 10 top left: Carl Palasota, carlpalasota@cox.net; 10 top right: Dirk Stennick Design; Patty Glikbarg, Pannagan Designs; 10 bottom left: Fox-Nahem Interior Design; 12: Pete Dieckhoff and Dean Read, Dean Read Architects; 13 right: Francesca Quagliata, 4th Street Design, www.4thstreetdesign.com; 14 center: Lee Kleinhelter/Pieces, www.piecesinc.com; 15: Kevin Price, J.A.S. Design-Build, www.jasdesignbuild.com; 19 bottom left and bottom right: Christian Liagre Interior Design; 20–21: Laura Del Fava, www.delfavastyle.com; 22: Waldo Fernandez; 23: Vanessa Murphy; 24: Olexo Architecture & Landscape; Kathy Farley, Artdecor; 25 right: Tim Clarke, Tim Clarke Design; 26: Tim Clarke, Tim Clarke Design; 30 top: Ellis A. Schoichet, EASA Architecture, www.easaarchitecture.com; Bess Wiersems and Megan Matthews, Studio 3 Design, www.studio-three.com; 38: John Lum Architecture, www.johnlumarchitecture.com; 39 top right: T. S. Hudson Interiors; Linda Woodrum, George Graves, Architect; 40 top left: Architect: Thomas Bateman Hood Architects, www.thomasbatemanhood.com; Interior Designer: Joseph Hittinger Designs, www.josephhittingerdesigns.com; 40 top right: Ricardo Legoretta, Architect & Designer; 40 bottom left: Tim Clarke, Tim Clarke Design; 41: Dirk Stennick Design; Patty Glikbarg, Pannagan Designs; 43 top right: Carl Palasota, carlpalasota@cox.net; 45 top right: Alexandra Champalimaud; 45 bottom left: Rosemary Wells, Viridian Landscape Architecture, www.vlastudio.com; 45 bottom right: Design: Paul Davis, Paul Davis Architects, www.pauldavisarchitects.com; Interior Design: Cheryl Burke Interior Design, www.cherylburkedesign.com; 47 left: Lee Kleinhelter/Pieces,

www.piecesinc.com; 48 bottom right: Interior Design: PhillipSides Interior; Architecture: Harrison Design Associates; 55 bottom: Interior Design: Steven Gambrel; Architecture: Historical Concepts; 58: Builder/Developer: Summerhill Homes, www.summerhillhomes.com; Designer: Kelly Barthelemy Design; 60 top right: Ricardo Legoretta, Architect & Designer; 60 bottom: Lee Kleinhelter/Pieces, www.piecesinc.com; 62: Architect: Thomas Bateman Hood Architects, www.thomasbatemanhood.com; Interior Designer: Joseph Hittinger Designs, www.josephhittingerdesigns.com; 66: Michael Bruno; 68 top: Heather Chadduck; 69: Jonathan Adler; 70: Architect: John Lum Architecture, johnlumarchitecture.com, Interior Design: Christopher Nordquist; 71 top left: Carl Palasota, carlpalasota@cox.net; 72 bottom left and bottom right: Randall Koll; 73: Adam Blackman/David Cruz; 75 top left: Christianna Coop; 77, 78: Carl Palasota, carlpalasota@cox.net; 79 top: Steven Kanner, Architect; 79 bottom: Fox-Nahem Interior Design; 80 top: Architect: Carol Cozen; Designer: Randy Weinstein; 82: Architect: Thomas Bateman Hood Architects, www.thomasbatemanhood.com; Interior Designer: Joseph Hittinger Designs, www.josephhittingerdesigns.com; 83 bottom left: Builder/Developer: Summerhill Homes, www.summerhillhomes.com; Designer: Kelly Barthelemy Design; 84 bottom: Tichenor-Thorpe, Architects; 85 top right: Design: Paul Davis, Paul Davis Architects, www.pauldavisarchitects.com; Interior Design: Cheryl Burke Interior Design, www.cherylburkedesign.com; 86–87: Michael K. Bell Interior Design. Inc., mkbellid@aol.com; 88–89: Waldo Fernandez; 90–91: Architect: Carol Cozen, cozenarchitecture.com; Designer: Randy Weinstein; 92–93: Carl Palasota, carlpalasota@cox.net; 94–95: Tim Clarke, Tim Clarke Design; 98: Design: Paul Davis, Paul Davis Architects, www.pauldavisarchitects.com; Interior Design: Cheryl Burke Interior

Design, www.cherylburkedesign.com; 102 bottom right: Carl Palasota, carlpalasota@cox.net; 106 top left: Michelle Kaufmann Designs, www.michellekaufmann.com; 106 bottom left: Shane Reilly; 106 bottom right: Charles De Lisle, De Lisle, Philpotts & Staub Interiors, www.dpsinteriors.com; 108: Charles De Lisle, De Lisle, Philpotts & Staub Interiors, www.dpsinteriors.com; 110: Michael K. Bell Interior Design. Inc., mkbellid@aol.com; 111 top right and bottom left and: John Lum Architecture, www.johnlumarchitecture.com; 111 bottom right: Charles De Lisle, De Lisle, Philpotts & Staub Interiors, www.dpsinteriors.com; 112–113: Pamela Skaist-Levy; 114–115: Robin Bell, Robin Bell Design, www.robinbelldesign.com; 116–117: John Lum Architecture, www.johnlumarchitecture.com; 118–119: Donlyn Lyndon; Placewares + Lyndon Design, www.lyndondesignstudio.com; 120–121: Carmen Mateo, Brand Kitchens & Design, www.brandkitchens.com; 122–123: Charles De Lisle, De Lisle, Philpotts & Staub Interiors, www.dpsinteriors.com; 124–125: Heather Chadduck; 126–127: Charles De Lisle, De Lisle, Philpotts & Staub Interiors, www.dpsinteriors.com; 128–129: Architect: Thomas Bateman Hood Architects, www.thomasbatemanhood.com; Interior Designer: Joseph Hittinger Designs, www.josephhittingerdesigns.com; 131: John Schneider and Kim Clements, J.A.S. Design-Build, Seattle; www.jasdesignbuild.com; 132: Pamela Hill & Lois MacKenzie, Otto Baat Group,

www.ottobaat.com; 133 top: Pamela Hill & Lois MacKenzie, Otto Baat Group, www.ottobaat.com; 133 bottom left, bottom right: Laura Del Fava, www.delfavastyle.com; 135: John Schneider and Kim Clements, J.A.S. Design-Build, Seattle; www.jasdesignbuild.com; 136: Bobby Webb; 140–141: Pamela Skaist-Levy; 146–147: Architect: John Lum Architecture, www.johnlumarchitecture.com, Interior Design: Christopher Nordquist; 148–149: Charles De Lisle, De Lisle, Philpotts & Staub Interiors, www.dpsinteriors.com; 152–153: Tia Zoldan, Zoldan Interiors; www.zoldaninteriors.com; 156: Ashley Hayley; 160: Lisa Rowe, Lisa Rowe Design; lisarowedesign@yahoo.com; 162 bottom right: Casa Midy, Jorge Almad and Anne-Marie Midy; 163: Lee Kleinhelter/Pieces, www.piecesinc.com; 167: Peter Dunham Interior Design; 168–169: John Lum Architecture, www.johnlumarchitecture.com; 170–171: Yolo Colorhouse, www.yolocolorhouse.com; 172–173: Charles De Lisle, De Lisle, Philpotts & Staub Interiors, www.dpsinteriors.com; 174, 175 top, 175 bottom left: Christopher Nordquist; 175 bottom right: Architect: John Lum Architecture, www.johnlumarchitecture.com, Interior Design: Christopher Nordquist; 180–181: Kenneth Brown; 182–183: Peter Dunham Interior Design; 184–185: John Lum Architecture, www.johnlumarchitecture.com; 187: Francesca Harris, FHIG, www.fhig.net; 192: Mark Marcinik, Greenmeadow Architects

Index